THE TEN COMMANDMENTS

—— "NAILED TO THE CROSS" *OR* ——
REQUIRED FOR SALVATION?

by David C. Pack
with George C. Rogers

For every cause there is an effect. Obeying the Ten Commandments identifies the cause that will produce every good and desirable effect.

But the world has been deceived, thinking that this great Law is burdensome and harsh, and lacks love and mercy. Yet, the world ignores the plain Word of God: "For this is the love of God, that we keep His commandments and His commandments are *not grievous*" (I John 5:3).

The Ten Commandments are NOT done away! Now you can learn why YOU should keep this living, active, spiritual Law of God.

TABLE OF CONTENTS

Introduction

God has created and sustained the universe with hundreds of billions of galaxies, each consisting of hundreds of millions of stars. Every movement of celestial bodies within these galaxies adheres to the laws of physics and chemistry. From the forces that bind atomic nuclei to the principles that govern these great star systems, God's laws regulate everything. From the fullness of the earth to the vastness of space, from the breathtaking beauty of the creation to the minds that can comprehend it, all testify to God's majesty and boundless creative forethought.

The brilliant scientist Albert Einstein observed the order, laws and forethought that God put into His creation. While he doubted the Bible's authority, he was convinced of the existence of a superior intelligence at work in the universe. Einstein believed there was a "god" who is revealed in the order and harmony of what existed. He was amazed at the harmony of natural laws, which revealed an intelligence of such superiority that the collective thinking of human beings was utterly insignificant (from *Out of My Later Years*, 1950).

The physical creation of Earth and the universe reflects order due to perfect interaction, balance and harmony with natural laws. Likewise, there exist *spiritual laws*, which, if obeyed, would ensure peace, harmony and fulfillment among men and nations. But the masses have not understood those laws.

God has allowed humanity to exercise free moral agency. After having violated God's spiritual laws throughout the course of human history, man will be forced to realize and appreciate that God's ways infinitely exceed his own. Six thousand years of agony stand in stark testimony to man's track record in living contrary to the laws of God, set in motion for man's own good.

The Ultimate Standard

The Ten Commandments are the core of the laws of God. Many scriptures expand upon them, and in great detail. God's commands are the universal standard that enables us to know when we are on course and when we have drifted from it.

The Bible—which defines every crucial principle and law governing life—is the standard in directing our paths. Psalm 119:9 states, "Wherewithal shall a young man cleanse his way? By taking heed thereto according to Your *word*." Verse 105 adds, "Your *word* is a lamp unto my feet, and a light unto my path."

Throughout history, navigators sailing the high seas have used the Big Dipper to locate the North Star. Once located, it revealed their orientation and heading. Other navigational instruments provided more details and assistance. In the same way, the Ten Commandments are the standard by which all human beings establish and maintain their bearing. They define the boundaries that people require in order to build and develop godly character.

Law Like No Other

But the Law of God is much more than a navigational instrument, and the Old Testament presents many verses with God's view of a Law that many believe to have become null and void in the New Testament "dispensation." Let's look at just a few passages, and as you read them ask yourself if they sound like a law that God would later render obsolete—one kept *for* people—fulfilled on their behalf by Christ—as many so willingly believe.

First, also consider verse 172 of Psalm 119 in which the psalmist recorded, "For all Your commandments are *righteousness*." Verse 18 adds this: "Open you mine eyes, that I may behold *wondrous things* out of Your law."

Now notice these almost never-mentioned statements of David in Psalm 19: "The Law of the LORD is *perfect, converting* [restoring] *the soul*" (vs. 7) and "the commandment of the LORD is *pure, enlightening the eyes*" (vs. 8).

How can anyone think that God would discard such a marvelous law? Those who believe the law is "done away," or "nailed to the cross," have a great deal of trouble trying to explain why God would abandon a law described in such glowing terms. The problem of "spiritualizing away" God's Law grows even more difficult when one considers just a few other statements.

For instance, let's place a couple of passages side by side, the first from the book of Ecclesiastes. Solomon concluded twelve fascinating, insightful chapters about life with what is of central importance for every human being: "Let us hear the conclusion of the whole matter: Fear God, and keep His commandments: for *this is the whole...man*" (12:13). Ask: Recognizing this could only be referencing the Ten Commandments because it is recorded in the Old Testament, how could such a powerful, comprehensive and conclusive statement no longer have application? Notice that the very next verse warns, "For God shall bring every work into judgment, with every secret thing, whether it be good, or whether it be evil" (vs. 14).

Why, with such obvious connection to the Law of God in context, are not more people concerned with such sobering warnings?

Now look at an almost identical statement to Solomon's, reflecting what God wished from—and for—His people, the nation of Israel: "O that there were such an heart in them, that they would fear Me, and keep all My commandments *always*, that it might be well with them, and with their children *forever!*" (Deut. 5:29).

Now further ask: Why do not more Bible students recognize the seriousness of what is recorded in Proverbs 28:9?: "He that turns away his ear from hearing the law [again, this can only be referencing the Ten Commandments], even his prayer shall be abomination." This is a most serious statement.

Many other passages could be added to this briefest of lists. (A chapter near the end of the book will look closely at various *New Testament* scriptures about law and sin.) Like the physical laws governing the universe, making all things run smoothly, the Ten Commandments are laws that govern a Christian's life, producing the true peace, real happiness, and ultimate success that all seek.

Did the Ten Commandments Precede Moses?

Most leaders of professing Christianity insist that the core of God's spiritual Law—the Ten Commandments—is done away. Repeating what they have been taught without requiring proof, they call it the "law of Moses" and claim that it was abolished by Jesus Christ's sacrifice. But they do not know the difference between the Levitical sacrificial rituals, the law of Moses and the law of God.

A combination of ignorance and an attempt to minimize the Ten Commandments as "dispensational" (obligatory for a limited period of time) has caused most to believe the Ten Commandments did not exist prior to Moses receiving them on Mount Sinai. Is this true? Is this what the Bible teaches? While other chapters of this book will address whether the New Testament requires obedience to these marvelous laws, our purpose here is to examine the period from Creation to Moses. Keeping in mind that scripture cannot be broken, what scriptures can be examined for proof?

Law of Moses or God's Law?

The Ten Commandments were never referred to as the law of Moses, but rather the law of God. First, understand this! The law of Moses consisted of (1) the civil laws, which were statutes and judgments that Moses relayed to the people from God, recorded in Exodus 21-23 and in the remaining books of the law, and (2) the ritualistic laws (or Greek: *ergon*) that were added later, summarized in Hebrews 9:10. They were ordinances regulating the job of the tribe of Levi in temple service, sacrifices (Leviticus 1-7) and associated functions. The word *ergon* means "works," as in the "works of the law" (such as in Galatians 2:16). This refers to the labor involving the Levitical rituals that were abolished by Christ's sacrifice.

The Ten Commandments were already in force long before they were officially given to Israel at Mount Sinai and this will be demonstrated. In fact, these commandments have existed since the creation of man. The Ten Commandments were never part of the law of Moses (addressed more fully later in the chapter) or the Levitical sacrificial system. The civil laws and sacrifices were *based on* God's commands, which constitute the core of His laws. Thus, the Ten Commandments precede and transcend any and every lesser law or practice based upon them—statutes, judgments, precepts, and ordinances.

The Ten Commandments are God's spiritual laws (Rom. 7:12, 14). They are just as active as the physical laws of gravity and inertia. Just as breaking physical laws results in physical consequences, breaking spiritual laws results in spiritual consequences.

Sin Defined

Most human beings either do not know of or do not like to be reminded of I John 3:4, which defines sin: "Whosoever commits sin transgresses also THE LAW: for sin is the *transgression* of THE LAW." As the subject develops, you will come to see (in stages) the central connection between sin and the law.

Romans 6:23 states that "the wages of SIN is *death*." Romans 5 explains, "Wherefore, as by one man sin entered into the world, and death by sin; and so death passed upon all men, *for that all have sinned*: (For until the law sin was in the world: but *sin is not imputed when there is no law. Nevertheless death reigned from Adam to Moses*, even over them that had not sinned after the similitude of Adam's transgression, who is the figure of Him that was to come)" (vs. 12-14).

In other words, Adam sinned. Sin is not imputed—does not apply—where there is no *law* (carefully read Romans 4:15). Death reigned from Adam to Moses. (Remember, death is the penalty for sin, which is defined as the transgression of the law.) The only way that Adam and his descendants could sin—break God's spiritual law—is if God's Law *already existed!* Without this law in place, no one could be guilty of sin.

Instead of rejecting sin, modern religionists reject the law. They view the law as a burden—they want to be free from keeping it. But notice the key lessons found in Romans 7:7: "What shall we say then? Is the law sin? God forbid. No, I had not known sin, but by the law: for I had not known lust, except the law had said, You shall not covet." It is not the law that is at fault—and Paul is clearly citing one of the Ten Commandments—but sin. God reveals to us what sin is. He does this by His perfect law. On his own, man cannot discover God's perfect law. God has to reveal and teach it to us.

Man's First Sin

In the Garden of Eden, God talked to Adam and gave him clear, understandable instructions. Adam needed this. He was an adult with an adult mind, but God had to reveal to him the spiritual boundaries that Adam could not discover on his own, without breaking God's laws. Genesis 2:15 states, "And the LORD God took the man, and put him into the garden of Eden to dress it and to keep it. And the LORD God commanded the man, saying, Of every tree of the garden you may freely eat: but of the tree of the knowledge of good and evil, you shall not eat of it: for in the day that you eat thereof you shall surely die."

Adam was given instructions on how to maintain the garden. He was also commanded not to eat of the tree of the knowledge of good and evil (not to decide for himself what is right or wrong), and was told exactly what the penalty would be for disobeying this command. In effect, he was presented with what would be the same penalty described in the New Testament: "the wages of sin is death" (Rom. 6:23).

God revealed to Adam, and to his wife, Eve, right knowledge about how to live. But He gave them the freedom to decide whether or not they would follow His way. This was free moral agency, which God has given to all mankind.

Satan, in the form of a serpent, told Eve that if she took the fruit of the forbidden tree, "You shall not surely die: for God does know that in the day you eat thereof, then your eyes shall be opened, and you shall be as gods, knowing good and evil" (Gen. 3:4-5). Being gullible in the face of Satan's shrewd tactics, Eve fell for his deception and ate from the tree, as did Adam.

Adam sinned by acting against God's command. He broke God's Law. In doing so, he became the servant of the one whom he obeyed—Satan. This principle is explained in Romans 6:16: "Know you not, that to whom you yield yourselves servants to obey, his servants you are to whom you obey; whether of sin unto death, or of obedience unto righteousness?"

Whoever or whatever someone obeys and serves is his god. In this case, Adam and Eve broke the FIRST COMMANDMENT by *putting another god before the Creator God.* In doing so, they also broke the FIFTH COMMANDMENT, by *dishonoring their Parent,* in the sense that Adam was a created *son* of God (Luke 3:38). Their sin also involved *stealing* (the EIGHTH COMMANDMENT), in that they took something that was not theirs. Besides this, Eve *lusted* for the forbidden fruit. Lusting is coveting, which breaks the TENTH COMMANDMENT.

Breaking one commandment leads to breaking all of them. This is precisely what the apostle James expressed in James 2:10: "For whosoever shall keep the whole law, and yet offend in *one* point, he is guilty of *all*." God's laws are interrelated and intricately woven together—if you break one, you eventually break them all. Sin always spreads.

In Genesis 4, Adam's first son, Cain, became angry against his brother Abel, because God accepted Abel's sacrifice, but not Cain's. Notice how God admonished Cain in verses 6-7: "And the LORD said unto Cain, Why are you wroth [angry]? and why is your countenance fallen? If you do well, shall you not be accepted? and if you do not well, *sin* [impossible without the Law] lies at the door. And unto you shall be his desire, and you shall rule over him." Cain murdered and broke the SIXTH COMMANDMENT.

When someone is in the wrong frame of mind, sin does lie at the door, waiting to happen, because sinful thoughts lead to sinful actions. God commands us to rule over sin—to control those pulls and impulses to commit sin. Cain murdered Abel and lied to God about it. This is a direct violation of the NINTH COMMANDMENT, which forbids "bearing false witness against your neighbor." Cain had sinned and he knew it. This happened a few decades after Adam had first sinned. Adam and Eve's expanding family knew that sin was the breaking of God's Law, or God would not have held them accountable.

Other Commandments in Force Before Sinai

The Bible gives examples of each of the Ten Commandments being kept before Moses' time. When God called Jacob to return to Bethel, where God had appeared to him approximately 21 years before, Jacob warned his people, "*Put away the strange gods that are among you, and be clean, and change your garments: and let us arise, and go up to Bethel; and I will make there an altar unto God, who answered me in the day of my distress, and was with me in the way which I went*" (Gen. 35:2-3). Jacob knew that God forbade idolatry—breaking the SECOND COMMANDMENT. By telling his household to put away their idols, this fulfilled the principle in Proverbs 16:6, "By mercy and truth iniquity is purged: and by the fear of the LORD men depart from evil."

When Abram told King Abimelech that Sarah, his half sister and wife, was merely his sister, he lied—another breaking of the NINTH COMMANDMENT. Believing this, Abimelech sent for Sarah. Now notice Genesis 20:3-4, 6: "But God came to Abimelech in a dream by night, and said to him, Behold, you are but a dead man, for the woman which you have taken; for she is a man's wife. But Abimelech had not come near her: and he said, LORD, will you slay also a righteous nation?...And God said unto him in a dream, Yes, I know that you did this in the integrity of your heart; for I also withheld you *from sinning against Me*: therefore suffered I you not to touch her." In this situation, Abimelech would have committed adultery, which is a sin. He would have broken the SEVENTH COMMANDMENT.

When Joseph was tempted by the advances of Potiphar's wife, he "...refused, and said unto his master's wife, Behold, my master knows not what is with me in the house, and he has committed all that he has to my hand; There is none greater in this house than I; neither has he kept back any thing from me but you, because you are his wife: how then can I do this great wickedness, and *sin against God?*" (Gen. 39:8-9). Joseph was well aware that adultery was sin. This occurred about 250 years before the law was officially presented to Israel at Mount Sinai!

The Lesson of Manna

During their march to the Promised Land, God told the Israelites to gather their daily amount of manna each morning. On the morning before the weekly Sabbath there would be enough for both days. This was because no manna would appear on the Sabbath, God's day of rest. God intended that the Israelites rest on the Sabbath, rather than spend time gathering manna. This account is given in Exodus 16. In verse 28, after some of the people deliberately broke the Sabbath by attempting to gather manna, God told Moses, "How long refuse you [Israel] to keep *My commandments and My laws?*"

Now notice verses 29-30: "See, for that the LORD has given you the Sabbath, therefore He gives you on the sixth day the bread of two days; abide you every man in his place, let no man go out of his place on the seventh day. So the people rested on the seventh day." So, the FOURTH COMMANDMENT was in effect *before* the Law was given at Mount Sinai.

By the time Israel entered the land of Canaan, the nations there had "run the full course"—they had surpassed the threshold of moral collapse, much like nations have done today. God knew that this would happen and had told Abram about it, over 400 years earlier: "And you shall go to your fathers in peace; you shall be buried in a good old age. But in the fourth generation they [Abram's seed—the nation Israel] shall come here again: for the iniquity of the Amorites is not yet full" (Gen. 15:15-16).

Here, the word "iniquity" comes from the Hebrew word *avon*, which means "perversity, mischief or sin." If there had been no law in force, there would not have been any iniquity or sin for the Amorites, or any other nation, to commit. Refer to Leviticus 18:3, 19-30 for more description of the iniquity and abominations committed by the Canaanites. They included sacrificing—murdering—their children in the fire of the false god Molech, every form of adultery and sexual perversity, and profaning the name of God, among other sins.

Take a look at the pre-Flood world: "And God saw that the wickedness of man was great in the earth, and that every imagination of the thoughts of his heart was only evil continually" (Gen. 6:1-3, 5-6). The word "wickedness" used here comes from the Hebrew word *rah*, which means "exceedingly evil." So wicked was mankind that verse 6 tells us, "And it repented the LORD that He had made man on the earth, and it grieved Him at His heart." This wickedness brought every conceivable type of sin and blatant disregard for the sanctity of life.

These sins were imputed—pointed out—by the laws of God—the Ten Commandments, which existed from the creation of mankind.

These examples show that *all* the Ten Commandments preceded Moses. From Adam to Moses, all men had sinned—had broken God's laws, the Ten Commandments. That is why God commended Abraham, saying, "Abraham *obeyed My voice, and kept My charge, My commandments, My statutes and My laws*" (Gen. 26:5).

The Law of God Is Given

God gave the Ten Commandments to ancient Israel, the physical "Church in the wilderness" (Acts 7:38), at Mount Sinai, in 1443 B.C. On the same date (the Day of Pentecost), in A.D. 31, God gave His Holy Spirit to the New Testament Church. This made it possible to obey God's perfect law. It is no coincidence that both events fell on the same day. They are intricately tied together, because the Holy Spirit is essential for keeping the Ten Commandments. Without it, carnal minds cannot obey God (Rom. 8:7-9).

Now consider Matthew 19:16-19: "And, behold, one came and said unto Him, Good Master, what good thing shall I do, that I may have eternal life? And He said unto him, Why call you Me good? There is none good but One, that is, God: but *if you will enter into life, keep the commandments.* He said unto Him, Which? Jesus said, You shall do no murder, You shall not commit adultery, You shall not steal, You shall not bear false witness, Honor your father and your mother: and, You shall love your neighbor as yourself."

The last six commandments (five are cited here) summarize love and concern toward other people: "You shall love your neighbor as yourself."

Many wrongly assume that the Old Testament makes little or no mention of love. They assume that Christ introduced for the first time the concept of *love* during *His* ministry, and that the God of the Old Testament was strict and harsh, lacking love and mercy. This assumption is wrong. They are also unaware that the God of the Old Testament was the One who later became Jesus Christ (see John 1:1-4, 14, John 8:56-58 and I Corinthians 10:4).

In fact, the Old Testament books of the Law—Genesis, Exodus, Leviticus, Numbers, Deuteronomy—build directly upon the principle of love. Here is what Deuteronomy states: "*And you shall love the LORD your God* with all your heart, and with all your soul, and with all your might" (6:5). This passage is the same as the original "Great Commandment," cited in Matthew 22:37. Love toward God is the first step to obedience within His Law.

How many people have been taught that the *Old* Testament stresses this?

Love toward neighbor is the second step in obedience to God. Leviticus 19:18 states, "You shall not avenge, nor bear any grudge against the children of your people, but *you shall love your neighbor as yourself*: I am the LORD." This admonition—what is the original "golden rule," came from Leviticus 19—straight from the Old Testament! It was *not* a new teaching first introduced in the New Testament, as most have erroneously believed.

Now notice Deuteronomy 10:19. It expands Leviticus 19:18: "*Love you therefore the stranger*: for you were strangers in the land of Egypt." God told Israel to not just tolerate foreigners among them, but to show them *mercy* and *consideration*. Human nature tends to suspect or hold in contempt those of different nationalities or races. God teaches otherwise. Finally, notice Leviticus 19:9-10: "And when you reap the harvest of your land, you shall not wholly reap the corners of your field, neither shall you gather the gleanings of your harvest. And you shall not glean your vineyard, neither shall you gather every grape of your vineyard; *you shall leave them for the poor and stranger*: I am the LORD your God."

Love, mercy, consideration—outgoing, outflowing concern for others—were all attributes possessed and taught by the God of the OLD TESTAMENT.

Let's return to Matthew 5. Verses 21-22 show how Christ "magnified" the Law, and made it "honorable" (Isa. 42:21), effectively expanding it and making it more binding than before. For instance, "You have heard that it was said by them of old time, You shall not kill; and whosoever shall kill shall be in danger of the judgment. But I say unto you, that whosoever is angry with his brother…shall be in danger of the judgment."

Just as this commandment was greatly expanded, so were all the others. Far from doing away with God's Law, Christ made it much more binding.

Some Background on the Ten Commandments

In ancient Israel, the Ten Commandments were the basis for: (1) Laws—rules of conduct established by authority; (2) Statutes—laws enacted by a law-making body or ruler; (3) Judgments—judicial decisions of court cases; (4) Ordinances—public decrees or regulations; by-laws of a municipality; religious ceremonies; (5) Precepts—authorized directions or orders; and (6) Covenants—binding agreements; which are formal sealed compacts, usually between two parties. These definitions should help you better understand many of the terms used in this book in relation to the law.

The Ten Commandments primarily governed individual conduct. The statutes governed national and religious affairs, such as observing the Holy Days. The judgments were based on the Ten Commandments and the statutes.

Most people have no idea that the Ten Commandments did not originate at Mt. Sinai. In fact, we saw that these laws had existed from the time God created Adam and Eve. By the time of Moses, the world had strayed so far from the truth that God had to again reveal His already long-existing laws and statutes to Israel. This is the real story of what happened at "Mt. Sinai."

The Old Covenant was a marriage agreement between God and the nation of Israel. God promised to provide for and bless her as long as she obeyed Him and kept His laws.

The Ten Commandments are actually categorized into two sections. The first four commandments define man's relationship to God. The last six define his relationship with his fellow human beings. This was also reinforced by Christ. Notice: "Then one of them, which was a lawyer, asked Him a question, tempting Him, and saying, Master, which is the great commandment in the law? Jesus said unto him, You shall love the LORD your God with all your heart, and with all your soul, and with all your mind. This is the first and great commandment. And the second is like unto it, You shall love your neighbor as yourself. On these TWO commandments hang all the law and the prophets" (Matt. 22:35-40).

Events Leading to Mount Sinai

During the time of Joseph, the children of Israel relocated to Egypt, where they remained for about two and a half centuries. Following the generation after Joseph's death, the Egyptians reduced the Israelites to slavery—just as God had revealed to Abraham (Abram) 400 years earlier (Gen. 15:12-16). Through a vision, God told Abram that his seed would become enslaved and oppressed in a land not their own. God also foretold that He would judge the nation that would enslave Israel and that His people would come out of their land with great substance. As this came to pass, God called Moses to fulfill an important role after He had specially prepared him throughout his lifetime.

To fully appreciate how Israel was miraculously delivered from Egypt, review the severity of slavery that they had suffered. Notice Exodus 2:23-25: "…the children of Israel sighed by reason of the bondage, and they cried, and their cry came up unto God by reason of the bondage. And God heard their groaning, and God remembered His covenant with Abraham, with Isaac, and with Jacob. And God looked upon the children of Israel, and God had respect unto them."

After Egypt had suffered nine catastrophic plagues, the tenth (the death of the firstborn of man and beast) proved to be the final, most devastating one. Afterwards, Israel plundered Egypt (on the following day portion of Passover) as multitudes of Egyptians lavished gifts and riches upon them, imploring them to leave, so that God would not completely destroy what was left. The millions of Israelites gathered together, according to their tribes. Of course, this took some time, since they were bringing with them all their belongings and animals.

Gathering to Leave

The night arrived (ushering in the First Day of Unleavened Bread). As Israel had gathered into one giant assembly, with the tribes organized into ranks, they started on their journey. (The number of tribes was originally twelve, having descended from the twelve sons of Jacob, later called Israel.) Among the Israelites was a company of other nationalities (probably mostly Egyptians) who opted to depart with them. The nation of Israel numbered about 600,000 men—or at least two and a half million people (and possibly up to 4 million), including women and children.

On this night (God later commanded it to be remembered and kept annually as the "Night to be Much Observed"), after the sun had set, a new phenomenon occurred. A huge cloud that was over the Israelites began to glow so brightly that it greatly exceeded the brightness of the full moon. This cloud would lead Israel through the wilderness, providing shade in the day and light in the night, for forty years. After a brief celebration, Israel left Egypt with a "high hand"—feeling the exhilaration of freedom, mixed with amazement at God's miracles.

After bringing Israel through the Red Sea, God destroyed Pharaoh's army, which had pursued them. Upon witnessing one of the most dramatic deliverances recorded in the Bible, Moses and the Israelites celebrated in song and praise. However, throughout the next few weeks, Israel complained—and this was in spite of witnessing the plagues in Egypt, being delivered at the Red Sea, and having the giant cloud pillar leading, shading and providing light.

Truly, human nature has a short memory regarding all things of God.

All Israel at Mt. Sinai

Prior to the giving of the Ten Commandments, Exodus 16 relates the account of how all Israel learned of the Sabbath. This had occurred a little over two weeks before they arrived at Mt. Sinai. Exodus 19:2 describes their arrival there. What a sight this must have been. Imagine this enormous "tent city" larger by far than most cities of today's world—and far bigger than the almost pitiful depictions so typical of Hollywood.

Then, shortly after Israel arrived at the base of Sinai, God summoned Moses to come up near the summit to receive instructions from Him.

Verse 3 describes Moses departing from the camp, answering God's call to ascend the mountain. As mentioned, God was about to enter into what is usually called the "Old Covenant" with ancient Israel. God told Moses about the covenant that He would make with Israel if they would agree to obey His laws. In this agreement, God would establish Israel as His nation among all nations of the earth.

His purpose was to be both Ruler and King of this national theocracy, to be ruled solely by God, apart from any kind of humanly-devised government. There were to be no elections, parliaments or congress, and no leaders apart from those God would directly appoint.

God's instruction to Moses was "Now therefore, if you [all of Israel] will *obey* My voice indeed, and keep *My covenant*, then you shall be a peculiar treasure unto Me *above all people*: for all the earth is Mine: and you shall be unto Me a kingdom of priests, and an holy nation. These are the words which you shall speak unto the children of Israel" (vs. 5-6).

Note this well. It was at this point that the *twelve* tribes of Israel were to become God's "chosen people." You have often heard the term. We could ask: Why then do so many believe that the Jews (only *one* tribe—Judah) are God's chosen people? Why are the other eleven tribes continually left out—forgotten—in the story of how God gave the Ten Commandments to Israel? (The incredible story of the twelve tribes of Israel, and who are their modern descendants, is described in our vital book *America and Britain in Prophecy*.)

After Moses departed from his meeting with God, he then gathered the elders and presented the terms of the covenant, which they accepted. Notice: "And Moses came and called for the elders of the people, and laid before their faces all these words which the LORD commanded him" (vs. 7). Moses then relayed this to God, and God told him to have the people wash their clothes and prepare to come before Him on the third day.

The Stage Is Set

The moment of truth had come. The agreement—God's covenant with Israel—was about to be struck, *if* the people agreed to God's terms. What was the people's response?

Notice again: "And all the people answered together, and said, All that the LORD has spoken WE WILL DO." It was Moses' responsibility to take the people's decision back to God: "And Moses returned the words of the people unto the LORD" (vs. 8).

This was a truly historic moment. The people of Israel agreed to accept God's leadership—to obey His Law, His rule—over them. Here was a veritable ocean of people (perhaps 40 times the number who could fit into a giant football stadium seating 100,000) prepared to obey God.

After three days, the entire assembly of Israel was to be prepared to meet God at the base of Mt. Sinai to receive His Law (vs. 11). As that day arrived (the same day that God's people today observe the Day of Pentecost), the people were apprehensive. They were instructed not to come too close to the mountain—to God's presence—or they would die. This was a most serious moment! As thick dark clouds enveloped the top of the mountain, intense lightning flashed and roaring thunder echoed between the mountains. The valley was filled with jolting and awesome sights and sounds. The Bible describes that God came with tremendous THUNDER and LIGHTNING—and great POWER and GLORY, to show Himself as the great God. It must have seemed that the noise level could not possibly increase. But then came the long, piercing, yet clear blast of a GREAT TRUMPET, which caused everyone, including Moses, to tremble: "And so terrible was the sight, that Moses said, I exceedingly fear and quake" (Heb. 12:21).

God was then ready to announce the Ten Commandments—the core of the covenant that He would make with Israel (Ex. 20:1-17; Deut. 5:6-21).

Imagine the deafening VOICE OF GOD (simply described as "exceeding loud")—booming with enough volume that, without amplification, millions could hear it! Notice further in Exodus 19: "And Moses brought forth the people out of the camp to meet with God; and they stood at the nether part of the mount. And mount Sinai was altogether on a smoke, because the LORD descended upon it in fire: and the smoke thereof ascended as the smoke of a furnace, and the whole mount quaked greatly" (vs. 17-18).

Picture it. The entire event must have been a stunning, goose-bump-raising, ear-splitting, blinding experience! It was in *this* setting that God chose to give His holy, righteous, perfect, spiritual LAW!

God Gives *HIS* Law

It is at this point in the account that so many go terribly wrong. Most professing Christians have been taught that *Moses* gave—or brought—the Ten Commandments. This has been a means of diminishing God's Law into merely the "law *of Moses*."

Here is what really happened in this perhaps most famous of all Bible accounts. Exodus 20 describes the giving of GOD'S great Ten

Commandments. Again, *who* gave them?: "And GOD spoke all these words, saying…" (vs. 1). This was clearly *God's* Law, *God's* TEN COMMANDMENTS—not Moses' or anyone else's. (What follows are the Ten Commandments – vs. 2-17.)

Deuteronomy 5 is Moses' later recounting to Israel of how God's Law was given: "The LORD talked with you *face to face* in the mount out of the midst of the fire, (I stood between the LORD and you at that time, to show you the word of the LORD: for you were afraid by reason of the fire, and went not up into the mount;) saying…" (vs. 4-5). God's voice then thundered out the Ten Commandments (vs. 6-21).

Yes, Moses did stand in front of the people as a kind of buffer to their fear of God's presence. But he did not give the Law—*GOD* gave His Law directly to Israel, "face to face." That is what it says. It was God's Law, and *HE* gave it. Now notice all-important verse 22: "These words *the LORD spoke unto all your assembly* in the mount out of the midst of the fire, of the cloud, and of the thick darkness, with a great voice: AND HE ADDED NO MORE. And He wrote them in two tables of stone, and delivered them unto me." We will momentarily revisit this passage.

This verse clearly shows that God spoke "unto all your assembly." This is plain. The Ten Commandments were given to Israel *by God*, not Moses! But there is this additional key phrase within the verse—"and He added no more."

The Law Was Complete

Other arguments have been raised by skeptics, would-be "theologians" and others who refuse to obey God, trying to connect the Ten Commandments to the various other statutes, ordinances, sacrifices, judgments and even the annual Feast days, which God commanded Israel to keep in Leviticus 23.

All of the other laws that God gave *later*—His statutes, ordinances, precepts and judgments—were not part of His *complete spiritual Law* given by Him directly to the people at Mt. Sinai. This must be understood, and so few people seem to recognize this. God held nothing back in the giving of His Law. He left nothing out—His spiritual Law was perfect and complete.

God's Law is *living*. Speaking of this Law, Acts 7:38 states, "This is he [Moses], that was in the *church in the wilderness* with the angel [Christ] which spoke to him in the mount Sinai, and with our fathers: who received the lively oracles to give UNTO US." That's right! God's Law is a living—"lively"—Law, and it was intended to be carried down "TO US."

The Ten Commandments are binding on God's people today—"US." They have not been done away. They were sent "unto us."

Have you ever noticed the following passage *from the New Testament?* The foundation—His Law—of God's Old Covenant agreement with Israel is the same as His New Covenant agreement with the Church: "For this is the covenant that I will make with the house of Israel after those days, says the Lord; I will put MY LAWS into their mind, and write them in their hearts: and I will be to them a God, and they shall be to Me a people" (Heb. 8:10).

We have now painted a dramatic picture of the setting in which God gave the Ten Commandments to the nation of Israel. This background sets the stage for understanding this great Law, and how it was ultimately sent to the entire world—for any who will choose to obey it!

The Ten Commandments and "Book of the Law" Are Different

Most people have no idea how to *prove* the Ten Commandments are completely different from the "book of the Law," or the Law of Moses. This is at least partly because they do not realize a series of verses, when put in correct sequence, leave no question that these were two *entirely separate laws*. This chapter is not complete without examining six final passages.

Deuteronomy 5 laid the groundwork with verse 22, just quoted, in which Moses was recounting the receiving of the Law of God to the assembled Israelites. After referencing in verse 3 the covenant God made, remember that *at that time* God "added no more," and that He "wrote them in two tables of stone, and delivered them unto me."

Next, let's plainly recognize that Moses also was used to bring a law. Notice, this time from Deuteronomy 33: "Moses commanded us a law, even the inheritance of the congregation of Jacob" (verse 4).

The Ark of God—and What Was "in" It

Now we go to chapter 10 of Deuteronomy, where Moses is recounting more of what happened. The role of the ark of God is introduced.

Read carefully: "At that time [when the Ten Commandments were first given] the LORD said unto me, Hew you two tables of stone like unto the first, and come up unto Me into the mount, and make you an ark of wood. And I will write on the tables the words that were in the first tables which you broke, and you shall put them *in* the ark. And I made an ark of shittim wood, and hewed two tables of stone like unto the first, and went up into the mount, having the two tables in mine hand. And he wrote on the tables, according to the first writing, the ten commandments, which the LORD spake unto you in the mount out of the midst of the fire in the day of the assembly: and the LORD gave them unto me" (vs. 1-4).

Then, I Kings 8:9 removes all doubt about whether anything else went into the ark. This is vital to establish before continuing: "There was nothing *in* the ark save the two tables of stone, which Moses put there at Horeb, when the LORD made a covenant with the children of Israel, when they came out of the land of Egypt."

The "Side" of the Ark

At this point, an all-important distinction can be made. The ark was very specially constructed so that a second and different law could be accommodated. Let's see what that law was and where it was kept. We return to Deuteronomy: "And it came to pass, when Moses had made an end of writing the words of this *law in a book*, until they were finished, that Moses commanded the Levites, which bare the ark of the covenant of the LORD, saying, take this *book of the law*, and put it in the *side* of the ark of the covenant of the LORD your God, that it may be there for a witness against you" (31:24-26). This reveals that the ark contained a separate compartment—actually a kind of pouch—on the "side" wherein was kept the longer book of the law.

It should now be clear that the Ten Commandments—*God's Law*—and the much longer book of the law—recorded by *Moses* (but even this was done on God's behalf)—are NOT the same sets of law. But let's remove all doubt with a final passage.

Here is what you should never forget: "Neither will I make the feet of Israel move any more out of the land…only if they will observe to do according to all that *I have commanded them*, AND according to all the law that my servant *Moses commanded them*" (II Kings 21:8).

There remains no doubt that God's Ten Commandments and Moses' book of the law, though certainly related, were entirely separate. Even the ark made this plain distinction.

Now for the Law of God...

The First Commandment— "No Other Gods Before Me"

The earth trembled as God began to speak. Moses later recorded, "And God spoke all these words, saying, I am the LORD your God, which have brought you out of the land of Egypt, out of the house of bondage. YOU SHALL HAVE NO OTHER GODS BEFORE ME" (Ex. 20:1-3). This is the FIRST COMMANDMENT.

The Bible reveals that this was not God the Father, but the LORD (*YHWH*, meaning the "Ever Living One" or "Eternal")—the Spokesman who later became Jesus Christ (John 1:1, 14).

The lightning, thunder, trumpet blast and earthquake that accompanied the receiving of the Ten Commandments were intended for a purpose: "And Moses said unto the people, Fear not: for God is come to prove you, and *that His fear may be before your faces, that you sin not*" (Ex. 20:20). As the people heard God's voice, they were ready to be obedient to every word. Yet history records that the memory of this event quickly faded from their minds.

The Only Place to Start

The all-important First Commandment establishes *Who* it was that gave these laws to ancient Israel in the wilderness. This command must be firmly established in your mind from the outset of your thinking about the Ten Commandments. When understood in its fullest context, it lies at the heart of all religion.

Surely, if the Bible is the inspired INSTRUCTION BOOK of an all-wise and all-powerful Creator God, who was also the *only true God* in the universe, His first commandment could not have been otherwise. Under no circumstances would that God want *other gods* worshipped in His place. In fact, in the very next commandment, the Author of these laws describes Himself as "a jealous God."

The God of the Bible leaves no room for doubt in the first *four* commandments. He expects to be worshipped *as He is*. He allows no room for confusion and does not want human opinion added—He accepts no substitution of the false for the true.

In fact, related to this, we can at least briefly reference the later discussed Fourth Commandment in an important context. The evolutionist has a big problem trying to explain belief in a God who created all life on earth in six days. Having rejected the Creation account of this God, it becomes much easier to go on to the next step—the very rejection of that God, and possibly the idea that there even is a God! Of course, faithful Sabbath observance *every seven days* would eliminate this problem.

(Though this is a separate element of the subject, you should also take time to prove that, in fact, there IS a God. Consider reading our informative booklet *Does God Exist?*, as well as our thorough, illustrated brochure *Evolution – Facts, Fallacies and Implications*. Unlike anything you have read, these help establish a foundation on which to confidently build a right relationship with God. Also note that a page recommending additional literature is included for the purpose of making the reader aware of material that greatly expands related subjects that cannot be as thoroughly discussed in this volume. At times, helpful literature will be referenced within the text.)

Begin With the Fear of the Lord

The First Commandment is the most basic requirement for beginning to understand God's truth and to fulfill our ultimate purpose. All humanity is warned to put God first, and to avoid false gods. The Being who issued that FIRST and GREAT commandment rephrased it in Matthew 22:37.

Notice: "Jesus said unto him, You shall love the LORD your God with all your heart, and with all your soul, and with all your mind. This is the first and great commandment." In this New Testament passage, Christ was essentially quoting the very words that He inspired in Deuteronomy 6:5!

The message of putting God *first* should ring loud and clear. Proverbs 9:10 tells all who will listen, "The fear of the LORD is the beginning of wisdom: and the knowledge of the holy is understanding." Psalms 111:10 adds, "The fear of the LORD is the beginning of wisdom: a good understanding have all they that do His commandments: His praise endures for ever."

Only by putting God first (in every area—worship, obedience and goals in life), is sound judgment and understanding accessible. King Solomon wrote, "Evil men understand not judgment: but they that seek the LORD understand all things" (Prov. 28:5). Another key proverb is Proverbs 1:7: "The fear of the LORD is the beginning of knowledge: but fools despise wisdom and instruction." Further notice Job 28:28: "And unto man He said, Behold, the fear of the LORD, that is wisdom; and to depart from evil is understanding."

Repetition is the best method to get a point across. The message of these scriptures should echo in our minds, just as God's voice echoed to Israel when He thundered these commandments.

Without starting in the right direction, everyone will ultimately reach the wrong destination. The First Commandment points mankind in the right direction from the very beginning. Notice what Paul observed concerning those who left God out of the picture: "Because that, when they knew God, they glorified Him not as God, neither were thankful; but became vain in their imaginations, and their foolish heart was darkened. Professing themselves to be wise, they became fools" (Rom. 1:21-22). Getting it right from the beginning is crucial. Also notice: "The wise men are ashamed, they are dismayed and taken: lo, they have rejected the word of the LORD; and what wisdom is in them?" (Jer. 8:9).

Another way of putting God first is portrayed in Matthew 6:31-34. Notice this: "Therefore take no thought, saying, What shall we eat? or, What shall we drink? Or, wherewithal shall we be clothed? (For after all these things do the Gentiles [all non-Israelites] seek:) for your heavenly Father knows that you have need of all these things. *But seek you first the kingdom of God, and His righteousness; and all these things shall be added unto you.* Take therefore no thought for the morrow: for the morrow shall take thought for the things of itself. Sufficient unto the day is the evil thereof." We can rely on this absolute promise—God always keeps His word.

Here is another vital key. Matthew 6:33 talks about seeking God's kingdom *and His righteousness*. But what *is* righteousness? Recall Psalm 119:172 defined it: "My tongue shall speak of Your word: for ALL YOUR COMMANDMENTS ARE RIGHTEOUSNESS." Certainly this means that we should OBEY these commandments!

Avoid False Gods

Some might think that obeying the First Commandment is relatively simple, since they do not worship statues of pagan gods. But you could easily violate it without realizing it. People who worship false gods are most often *oblivious* to that fact. Whatever occupies your interest and/or time more than anything else could well be *your* god. Idolatry, strictly speaking, is the worship of idols. But there is another less apparent form of idolatry. This is the blind or excessive devotion to anything. The object of such devotion becomes a false god and the blind devotee becomes an idolater.

Probably the "god" that people most often put before the true God is *money*. To many, the chance of winning a lottery or contest is their most treasured "religious experience." Playing the lottery is at an all-time high. Television commercials promote lotteries, sending people straight into fantasies. They buy tickets weekly, or even daily, sometimes leading to financial ruin.

Another false god that countless millions worship is politics. Some, especially conspiracy theorists, exalt their political ideology as a virtual religion. While there may be some credibility to many of these theories, people obsessed by them are blinded to God's purpose and plan of salvation. They only look at life through the narrow portal of their particular theory. Avoid anything that stands between you and the truth of God!

Many who fall into forms of liberalism generally oppose everything associated with God. Their *own ideology* is their false god, which credits evolution as the origin of all life. These people are generally the architects and producers of the secular, anti-religious media, which offer today's generation new depths of sex and violence, disguised as entertainment. Though elevated in university systems and controlling public education, liberal intellectuals almost invariably promote the opposite of God's truth.

Another pitfall that traps most people is an almost religious reverence for the medical field. A great many people show far more respect to doctors and hospitals than to God. Although the medical profession has its place and does fill a real need, many seem to stand in awe of each new medical breakthrough more than of the God who made the amazing human body. They place their trust and hope in the false gods of modern medicine and scientific research to deliver mankind from all sickness and disease. Again, not all medical breakthroughs and scientific research are bad, but it is a mistake to put hope and trust in this rather than God. As you draw closer to God, you will come to realize that much better results are possible by looking *to Him* for healing. God instructs His servants to seek His intervention in matters of healing (Jms. 5:14-15), and often describes Himself as the God that heals (Ex. 15:26).

It is important to understand that Jesus Christ carried out a dual ministry: (1) preaching the gospel of the kingdom of God and (2) healing the sick and casting out demons (see Luke 4:18 and Luke 7:22). The original apostles continued in this same pattern.

In contrast to the first century, healing today occurs primarily within the Church, rather than in dramatic public "healings." Pseudo-healers have made a mockery of healing, through circus sideshow fakery. Modern medicine may help treat the *effects* of disease, but only God can truly heal.

Others worship sports figures, entertainers or *themselves* in place of God.

Almost all turn to materialism, in one form or another, to fulfill their lives. Some turn to cars, others to clothing, and still others to a combination of every material thing they can possibly obtain. So many do this in a vain attempt to fill the void that exists within their lives—the absence of God's Holy Spirit.

Know the Real God

The most basic knowledge about the God of the Bible is almost universally lacking today. This is illustrated by just one survey done in 2008 that yielded an incredible finding. Only 62 percent of Jewish people believe that God is male. With a few of the other 38 percent saying He is female, most of the others profess they "do not know."

The way to know the real God of the Bible is to seek Him above all else. Read—study—the Bible alongside our literature. This will help you learn to fear and honor God. It will help you gain doctrinal understanding as you become better grounded in the truth. Your relationship with God also hinges upon your contact with Him in sincere, humble prayer. Read the Psalms on your knees in prayer just as if the words were your own. This will help make these words eventually become your own praise toward God. Try this with Psalms 19, 119 or various other chapters you find inspiring.

Ask God to instill within you a proper fear and respect for Him, beginning with His name. If you do this, you will come to view God with greater awe. Strive to fill your mind with uplifting thoughts on the wonders of His creation. Learn to appreciate His handiwork, such as the different kinds of trees, the unique designs of flowers, the incredible organization of beehives and the mysterious migration of birds. Think about the huge spiraling galaxies and remind yourself that God knows every individual star—countless billions of them— by name (Psa. 147:4). And determine to appreciate His incredible wisdom and forethought, which are reflected throughout His awesome creation. It daily testifies to His genius.

People who aspire to follow God, while enduring this hostile world, must be on guard not to allow anything to come between them and God. Be aware that human nature tends to set up false gods in place of the true God. Seek to honor and treasure God. Some people are reluctant to praise Him, due to the way pseudo-Christians resort to sanctimonious gyrations in their "worship." Do not allow this to stop you from learning to do this properly. We can praise God through proper hymns and private prayer. Learn the correct way to praise God, as David and others did in the Psalms and other scriptures. It will then be possible to praise God with your own original thoughts and words. Best of all, you will have been trained to praise God *as He has instructed*, not as pseudo-Christians do!

"You Shall Have No Other Gods Before Me"

The First Commandment and its immediate implications are also found in Deuteronomy 6:4-9: "Hear, O Israel: The LORD our God is one [the correct meaning is "only" or "alone"] LORD: and you shall love the LORD your God with all your heart, and with all your soul, and with all your might. And these words, which I command you this day, shall be in your heart: And you shall teach them diligently unto your children, and shall talk of them when you sit in your house, and when you walk by the way, and when you lie down, and when you rise up. And you shall bind them for a sign upon your hand, and they shall be as frontlets between your eyes. And you shall write them upon the posts of your house, and on your gates."

Human beings were designed to practice the Ten Commandments as a way of life. God commands that we also teach them to our children, discuss them and meditate upon them. A host of passages declare as much.

What If...?

Let's ask: what if the entire world kept the First Commandment? To begin with, there would be no false religion—none! If all humanity put the true God first, seeking His wisdom and guidance, then wrong or incomplete concepts in all areas of life would disappear. Over 99% of religion today is false, so there would be an immediate and DRAMATIC change all over the earth. As the world came to know and fear the true God, it would learn that His system of government and culture—and every aspect of civilization—should be followed. Mankind would look sincerely into His Word to seek true wisdom and understanding—and God would grant them.

By knowing and fearing the true God, the world would soon come to appreciate and obey the other nine commandments. The gospel of the kingdom of God has everything to do with Jesus Christ coming with the saints to rule the world, administering the laws of God to all nations. Today, only a relative few individuals are willing to truly worship the God of the Bible. They are now by *choice*, in effect, receiving, and experiencing, a sneak preview of the millennial rule of Christ—when the whole world will be *required* to obey the true God.

Finally, if the whole world kept only one of the Ten Commandments, this First Commandment would be the most important. Consider. Knowledge of the true God would lead them into every one of the other truths of God, including all the other commandments.

The Second Commandment— "You Shall Not Make Unto You Any Graven Image..."

The ancient nations, cut off from the real God, almost invariably worshipped idols. The masses needed gods near at hand—and this meant those that could be seen. So, in part because of the environment in which they lived, before God could instruct Israel how to properly worship Him, He first had to show them how *not* to worship Him.

Exodus 20:4-6 records the SECOND COMMANDMENT. Here is God's explicit directive: "YOU SHALL NOT MAKE UNTO YOU ANY GRAVEN IMAGE, or any likeness of any thing that is in heaven above, or that is in the earth beneath, or that is in the water under the earth: you shall not bow down yourself to them, nor serve them: for I the LORD your God am a jealous God, visiting the iniquity of the fathers upon the children unto the third and fourth generation of them that hate Me; and showing mercy unto thousands of them that love Me, and keep My commandments."

This commandment is a very broad, sweeping, explicit prohibition intended to cover *every* form of false worship involving *every* other kind of supposed "god," and representation of such, that human beings with creative human reasoning could devise. Like any parent whose children chose to come home to a different house and to different parents after school, the Parent who made all human beings— His children—*would* certainly be jealous if they went off after idols and false gods.

God specifically defined the forbidden ways that were used to worship idols. He realized human nature's tendency to justify loopholes around His instructions.

The First Commandment forbids having other gods before the true God. The Second Commandment forbids using an image to represent the true God, or *any* false god. This commandment deals specifically with using physical images for worship or as representations of anything related to worship. This does not condemn the existence of statues or pictures in general—only their use for worship. Therefore, using any statue or picture to represent God is expressly *forbidden*. Man is to worship, bow down to and serve the Creator God. God does not allow man to transfer this same honor to an image representing Him. He strongly warned Israel of this danger.

Notice God's specific instructions to Moses: "You shall not make with Me gods of silver, neither shall you make unto you gods of gold" (Ex. 20:23). These were God's *first words* to Moses after giving him the Ten Commandments!

Again, notice verses 5-6: "...for I the LORD your God am a jealous God, visiting the iniquity of the fathers upon the children unto the third and fourth generation of them that hate Me; and showing mercy unto thousands of them that love Me, and keep My commandments." If people persist in idol worship, God will not only punish *them*, but also their children, grandchildren, and great-grandchildren. No other commandment gives such detailed implications.

Plainly God hates idolatry—and directly equates it with hating Him!

However, Almighty God promises to bless those who love and obey Him! Individuals who choose to obey God will not be punished for their parents' disobedience.

God's Warnings to Israel

Leviticus 26:1 warns, "You shall make you no idols nor graven image, neither rear you up a standing image, neither shall you set up any image of stone in your land, to bow down unto it: for I am the LORD your God."

In turning away from worshipping such images, Israel went against the current of the surrounding nations, as well as their *carnal human nature*. The natural mind seeks for some image to represent the god it worships. Human nature finds it easier to worship a physical object than to worship the invisible God. But the Second Commandment forbids using images to even *assist* or *remind* in worshipping God.

Deuteronomy 4:15-20 expands upon this in greater detail: "Take you therefore good heed unto yourselves; for you saw no manner of similitude on the day that the LORD spoke unto you in Horeb out of the midst of the fire: lest you corrupt yourselves, and make you a graven image, the similitude of any figure, the likeness of male or female, the likeness of any beast that is on the earth, the likeness of any winged fowl that flies in the air, the likeness of any thing that creeps on the ground, the likeness of any fish that is in the waters beneath the earth: and lest you lift up your eyes unto heaven, and when you see the sun, and the moon, and the stars, even all the host of heaven, should be driven to worship them, and serve them, which the LORD your God has divided unto all nations under the whole heaven. But the LORD has taken you, and brought you forth out of the iron furnace, even out of Egypt, to be unto Him a people of inheritance, as you are this day."

Where in this command is there room for the near endless number of idols found on Earth today that appear in the very forms God here condemns?

The ancient Greeks worshipped, in their case, mostly images of men and women. Many of the nations around Israel worshipped images of various land, air and sea creatures, such as the Philistine fish god, Dagon. The Babylonians and others worshipped the "host of heaven"—the sun, moon and stars.

Here is how Moses warned Israel about idolatry: "Take heed unto yourselves, lest you forget the covenant of the LORD your God, which He made with you, and make you a graven image, or the likeness of any thing, which the LORD your God has forbidden you. For the LORD your God is a consuming fire, even a jealous God" (Deut. 4:23-24).

Israel's Track Record

How well did Israel listen to God's revealed instruction? In only a matter of days during Moses' absence, Aaron, under pressure from certain of the congregation, allowed them to mold a golden calf. The worship of the calf was followed by a celebration in which the people "sat down to eat and to drink, and rose up to play" (Ex. 32:1-6).

Judges 2 summarizes Israel's record for about three centuries after arriving in the Promised Land. Less than a generation after Joshua's death, a cycle began.. In departing from God, one of the first things that Israel adopted was idol worship.

Judges 17 and 18 record how low Israel had descended. A Levite named Micah had come to possess a "valuable" idol. He was elated to expand his collection of idols. Judges 17:6 shows the extent to which Israel had forgotten God's ways. Notice: "In those days there was no king in Israel, but *every man did that which was right in his own eyes.*"

Without God's Law, there exists no standard by which to live. Studying such accounts should help you appreciate the order and harmony that flow from obeying God's laws.

Psalms 78:56-58 records, "Yet they tempted and provoked the Most High God, and kept not His testimonies: but turned back, and dealt unfaithfully like their fathers: they were turned aside like a deceitful bow. For they provoked Him to anger with their high places, and *moved Him to jealousy with their graven images.*"

Pictures of "Christ"

God expressly forbids the use of any pictures or images to represent Him. Jesus Christ is now at the right hand of God the Father, serving as our High Priest. There is no justification for any images or pictures of Christ. Even pictures in general are forbidden to be worshipped. Israel was to destroy pictures and images belonging to the nations that occupied the Promised Land: "Then you shall drive out all the inhabitants of the land from before you, *and destroy all their pictures, and destroy all their molten images*, and quite pluck down all their high places" (Num. 33:52).

Pictures of Christ are often found in bibles and other literature, and on the walls of homes and churches. They are prominent in Protestant churches, as well as Catholic churches that take the extra step of adding statues of Christ and Mary. Not only are these pictures and images forbidden, those that supposedly represent Christ bear no resemblance whatsoever to the way He really appeared. For instance, we know that Christ was Jewish, as the Bible states: "For it is evident that our Lord sprang out of Judah" (Heb. 7:14). This is not the usual picture presented either by popular artwork or Hollywood.

Also, Christ is always depicted as having long hair. However, He inspired Paul to write, "Does not even nature itself teach you, that, if a man have long hair, it is a shame unto him?" (I Cor. 11:14). During Christ's time, the Romans typically had short haircuts. Statues exist today of various Romans and people of other races at that time, and their hair length was short.

Some confuse Christ's appearance with the Nazarites. This is because they confuse *Nazarites* with *Nazarenes*. Nazarites were those who took the Nazarite vow. They were not to cut their hair or beard during the time of their service (Num. 6:5). Upon completing their vow, they shaved their heads (Num. 6:18). Nazarenes were people who came from the town of *Nazareth*. The term Nazarite vow has nothing to do with the town in which Christ grew up.

Pictures of Christ existed as early as 400 years after His death. These "pictures" were paintings that artists conjured up to show how, supposedly, Jesus must have appeared. Not surprisingly, most all of these early painters were steeped in counterfeit Christianity.

This explains in part why, instead of portraying Christ as a Jew with short hair, the early images bore a remarkable resemblance to the Roman god Jupiter, who supposedly ruled over all the other gods. Jupiter was attributed to have overthrown his father, Saturn, taking over the rule of the world. This meshed perfectly with the theology of the counterfeit church, which portrayed Jesus as having now superseded the God of the Old Testament, whom they incorrectly identified as God the Father. False teachers portray the theology of Christ as vetoing the harsh rule of God the Father and replacing those "harsh Ten Commandments" with "tolerance and love."

The use of this image of Jupiter Olympus gained momentum, like all the other false doctrines the counterfeit church perpetuated. Today, people who think they worship Christ are worshipping something entirely different—in appearance as well as substance!

Recall that the Jews paid Judas Iscariot to lead them to Christ. Upon betraying Christ, Judas did not describe Him in the following manner: "Well, He has this sad, sanctimonious look and exceptionally long hair. He will probably be carrying a lamb on His shoulder and you just could not miss that glowing halo."

In reality, Christ looked like the average Jew of His day—so much so that Judas had to specifically identify Him by kissing Him. Like any carpenter of His time, Christ would have had a weather-seasoned, masculine appearance—not the soft features imagined by painters centuries later. The prophet Isaiah was inspired to record, "For He shall grow up before Him as a tender plant, and as a root out of a dry ground: He has no form nor comeliness [beauty, attractiveness]; and when we shall see Him, there is no beauty that we should desire Him" (53:2).

The world's concept of who and what Christ was is as false as its idea of what He actually looked like! (You may read our article "Did Jesus Have Long Hair?" for more detail.)

A Church Sanctions Idolatry

As an extension of the Babylonian Mysteries religion, the early Catholic church continued their centuries-old tradition of image worship. The true Church exposed the Catholics' blatant idolatry in the early centuries. In order to avoid condemnation and negative publicity, the Catholic church had to do one of two things: either cease this practice, or change the biblical laws regarding idolatry.

Not surprisingly, they chose the latter.

The theologian/scholar, Augustine (A.D. 354-430), enacted this change and "saved the day." This man carefully re-structured the Ten Commandments to minimize the incriminating indictment that the Second Commandment directly brought upon them.

The Second Commandment condemns image worship. Therefore, by "combining" the first and second commandments, Augustine essentially "did away" with the Second Commandment. In order to maintain a total of ten, he split the last commandment into two separate commands. This re-arrangement changed the Ninth Commandment to read, "You shall not covet your neighbor's wife," and the Tenth to read, "You shall not covet your neighbor's house."

After breaking from the Roman church, Martin Luther retained the Catholic texts of the Bible, including the Augustine division.

Notice the following quote from *The Encyclopedia Britannica*: "The Church of Rome and the Lutherans adopt the Augustine division...combining into one the first and second commandments of Philo, and splitting his tenth commandment into two" (*11th edition, Vol.7,* p. 907). Philo was an eminent Jewish scholar of the early first century. He advocated the proper division of the Ten Commandments, as they appear in the King James Version of the Bible.

In combining the first two commandments, Augustine blatantly altered the Ten Commandments. Also, the splitting of the Tenth

Commandment presents an unnatural and transparent attempt to alter God's Word. —

In Romans 13:9, Paul mentions all five of the last commandments and makes no distinction in the one forbidding coveting. In Romans 7:7, he states, "What shall we say then? Is the law sin? God forbid. No, I had not known sin, but by the law: for I had not known lust, except the law had said, You shall not covet." We would expect to find this intact as one commandment, since Augustine did not make the change until about 350 years after Paul's death.

If the Bible you are reading is a classic Catholic Bible, this will explain why the Ten Commandments, as listed from the King James Version, differ from your version. But not all Catholic versions contain this Augustine division. If your Bible does not include the Second Commandment in its true form, obtain a more objective, less corrupted version of the Bible. (You may also read our booklet *How We Got the Bible – Which Translations Are Best?*)

Now read the sobering instruction—charge!—of Deuteronomy 4:1-2: "Now therefore hearken, O Israel, unto the statutes and unto the judgments, which I teach you, for to do them, that you may live, and go in and possess the land which the LORD God of your fathers gives you. *You shall not add unto the word which I command you, neither shall you diminish aught from it*, that you may keep the commandments of the LORD your God which I command you." —

Why would Augustine and other theologians and scholars not fear to violate this direct command from God? Did they willingly violate it for the same reason that they defied the Sabbath commandment and most of the laws and statutes of God? (Read our booklet *Many Shall Come in My Name*.)

Did Israel Remain Faithful?

We could pause and ask whether the nation of Israel ultimately lived up to her promises to God made in the book of Exodus. And then we must briefly examine what can be learned from her record and how any lessons can be applied. You will see that the relevance to hundreds of millions alive today will be shocking—and unmistakable.

God intended that the nation of ancient Israel be a MODEL NATION that all other nations would copy. This was always His purpose. He expected His people to set an example for surrounding nations of how happiness, peace, abundance, blessings and protection from enemies would result from obedience to Him. Sadly, despite an early willing-ness and determination to obey God, starting when the command-ments were first given at Sinai, Israel repeatedly found herself *copy-ing* the nations around her and worshipping their gods, thus achieving the very opposite of God's purpose! (Recall how quickly Israel fell into worship of the "golden calf" after the Ten Commandments were given—before Moses could even get down from the mountain.) This worship of false gods had repercussions lasting thousands of years.

The long, broken history of Israel is that she turned from the true God and fell into the seductive trap of idolatry and the worship of foreign gods, doing this over and over again. Each time this pattern repeated itself, God sent her back into captivity and slavery. After a time, she would cry out in bondage, offering repentance, and God would raise up a judge and deliver her. But His people would quick-ly fall right back into the worship of false gods and idols, leading back to captivity, then to later repentance, again followed by God's merciful deliverance—all of this happening time and again. This cycle, described in the book of Judges and elsewhere, was never bro-ken until ancient Israel and Judah finally went into captivity (for the next-to-last time), with ten of the twelve tribes becoming lost to his-tory. Only the Jews—Judah mixed with one other tribe—have re-tained their national identity, and this is largely attributed to having continued to observe God's Sabbath.

Jeremiah and Isaiah Summarize

Here is how God, through the prophet Jeremiah, describes and la-ments the continual actions of His "nation"—His people: "Has a na-tion *changed their gods*, which are yet no gods? But My people have changed their glory for that which does not profit. Be astonished, O you heavens, at this, and be horribly afraid, be you very desolate, says the LORD. For My people have committed two evils; *they have forsaken Me* the fountain of living waters, and hewed them out cis-terns, broken cisterns, that can hold no water" (2:11-13).

The latter phrase in this passage accurately describes *all* the false gods devised by men and nations over the last 6,000 years. These man-made "gods"—made of wood, stone, metal and *false think-ing—are* truly "broken cisterns, that can hold no water." Yet, those nations (and religions) cleave to these fictional gods with a faithful-ness Israel never showed to the true God.

Jeremiah continues, describing Israel's approach to gods she had copied and created: "Saying to a stock [of wood—a mere carved idol], You are my father; and to a stone, You have brought me forth: for they have turned their back unto Me, and not their face." Speaking for God, Jeremiah then says of these gods, "but in the time of their trouble they will say, Arise, and save us. But where are your gods that you have made you? Let them arise, if they can save you in the time of your trouble: for according to the number of your *cities* are your gods, O Judah" (vs. 27-28).

This is a classic description of what is seen throughout the world in all the modern nations that consider themselves to be based upon Judaeo-Christian roots. Idols, carvings, religious statues and stained-glass windows abound on and in every church in every city, with no one thinking anything of it.

Even as early as the first century, the apostle Paul was warning a congregation of God's people (the Corinthians)—those of His Church!—of the danger of following "another Jesus," who is tied to "another gospel" and this, in turn, he revealed is tied to following "another spirit" (II Cor. 11:3-4). You will find this revelation to be positively stunning—shocking you beyond what you can possibly imagine about the traditional "Jesus" taught in almost every church throughout the Western World.

Now continuing with Jeremiah's account. God had always made Himself available to Israel, easy to find for those who sought Him: "O generation, see you the word of the LORD. Have I been a wilderness unto Israel? A land of darkness? Wherefore say My people, We are lords; we will come no more unto You? Can a maid forget her ornaments, or a bride her attire? Yet My people have *forgotten* Me days without number" (vs. 31-32). God has never been "a wilderness" to those who seek Him. The question has always been whether Israel would seek and obey Him.

How many young women would ever permit themselves to dress up for a special occasion, but forget to put on jewelry—her "ornaments"? Surely few. Then, what bride at her wedding could possibly forget to put on her wedding dress—her "attire"? Absolutely none.

Yet, astonishingly, Israel had forgotten THEIR GOD!

Of course, this was only able to happen because she disregarded God's basic instruction—and commandments!—and got involved with the gods of surrounding nations.

The prophet Isaiah declares this from God about the woeful—and ignorant—state of His people, then and today: "Hear, O heavens, and give ear, O earth: for the LORD has spoken, I have nourished and brought up children, and they have rebelled against Me. The ox knows his owner, and the ass his master's crib: but Israel does not know, My people do not consider. Ah sinful nation, a people laden with iniquity, a seed of evildoers, children that are corrupters: they have forsaken the LORD, they have provoked the Holy One of Israel unto anger, they are gone away backward" (1:2-4).

Isaiah is describing a nation that had fallen into every conceivable kind of corruption, evil and sin, all of which could be attributed to having forsaken the true God.

Worldwide Confusion—Gods and More Gods

The world is filled with gods of every sort. It is as though mankind has reserved the very best of its creative powers for the invention of every conceivable type of god and goddess—whether composed of physical matter or defined by ethereal concepts in the mind. The world's billions worship literally millions of gods.

The apostle Paul expresses it best as he introduces the true God of the Bible: "For though there be that are called gods, whether in heaven or in earth (as there be gods many, and lords many), but to us there is but one God, the Father, of whom are all things, and we in Him; and one Lord Jesus Christ, by whom are all things, and we by Him. Howbeit there is not in every man that knowledge..." (I Cor. 8:5-7).

The Romans worshipped and built temples to an almost endless array of gods and goddesses. But it is said that the ancient Greeks worshipped as many as 30,000 gods. Not to be outdone, the Hindus of today are said to have 5 million, including their own trinity consisting of Sheva, Brahma and Vishnu! Of course, the Egyptians, as did other civilizations, also had their own brand of a trinity—Osiris, Horus and Isis. Then there is Tao, Confucius, Buddha, Allah and a host of other gods, goddesses and idols, worshipped today, including totem poles, nature, snakes, animals and fish in the sea, volcanoes and mountains, fire, wind, rocks, sun, moon, planets, stars and even certain human beings who are considered to be divine. Again, then, there are all the different kinds of metaphysical concepts of gods adored and worshipped in the mind—some of which have been depicted by physical symbols and representations rendered by artists. This describes the trinity.

Yet, and most are probably not aware of this, vastly more people believe in the three-in-one god of modern Christianity than any other form of god.

The Unknown God

At this point, we need to look at a fascinating but longer passage that illustrates how superstitious mankind will worship almost anything, including worship of many gods at the same time to avoid possible offense to whatever god they may have overlooked. This account paints an astounding picture. Take careful note of the last sentence. The story from Acts involves Paul in Athens:

"Then Paul stood in the midst of Mars' hill, and said, You men of Athens, I perceive that in all things you are too superstitious. For as I passed by, and beheld your devotions [gods], I found an altar with this inscription, TO THE UNKNOWN GOD. Whom therefore you ignorantly worship, Him declare I unto you. God that made the world and all things therein, seeing that He is Lord of heaven and earth, dwells not in temples made with hands; neither is worshipped with men's hands, as though He needed any thing, seeing He gives to all life, and breath, and all things; and has made of one blood all nations of men for to dwell on all the face of the earth, and has determined the times before appointed, and the bounds of their habitation; that they should *seek* the Lord, if haply they might *feel after* Him, and *find Him*, though he be not far from every one of us: for in Him we live, and move, and have our being; as certain also of your own poets have said, For we are also his offspring. Forasmuch then as we are the offspring of God, we ought not to think that the Godhead is like unto gold, or silver, or stone, graven by art and man's device. And the times of this ignorance God winked at; *but now commands all men every where to repent*" (17:22-30).

Notice Paul's reference "TO THE UNKNOWN GOD" (also found in capital letters in the King James Bible). God had to reveal Himself to the superstitious Greeks through Paul. They had devised a "catch-all" inscription designed to include any other god missed in their "devotions." Paul took note of how they had covered themselves in their determination to leave no stone unturned in the worship of every deity. But they had not tried to "seek," "feel after" and "find Him."

King Solomon recorded that there is "no new thing under the sun" (Ecc. 1:9). Truly, the God of the Bible *has been unknown* to countless millions who have been content to worship a god *selected for them* by men. Theologians and religionists have sought the opinions of philosophers, scholars and supposed experts, instead of the only important opinion—that of God, found in His Word. We will see that, centuries ago, these religious leaders reported their findings to the masses who were only too willing to swallow what was presented to them—the trinity!—without proof.

The God Who Is Alive

Ultimately, we ask, What is the difference between the God of the Bible and all other gods? How does God Himself differentiate who and what He is from all others?

Throughout Scripture, God describes Himself over and over again as "the living God"—the "Eternal"—"I AM THAT I AM" (the name in Exodus 3:14 that Moses was instructed by God to use when representing Him to Pharaoh). In other words, the God of the Bible establishes who He is and separates Himself from all other gods by declaring Himself to be ALIVE!—LIVING!—meaning ALL other gods are non-existent or, in a sense, "dead." In effect, put another way, the true God states, "I AM," meaning other gods "are not"—period.

It is vital that the reader continually ask whether he or she is worshipping the ONE TRUE GOD—the God who is ALIVE—or something non-existent, inert and "dead," a god who *is not*! This question towers over all others presented in this volume.

Idolatry in Perspective

Without God's Spirit, the human mind is naturally inclined to worship images, simply because they are physical. Someone who breaks the First Commandment will eventually break the Second Commandment.

Satan the devil has capitalized upon this. He knows that breaking one commandment leads to breaking another. For example, in many pagan religions, adultery—violation of the Seventh Commandment—was actually part of the worship rituals.

A true worshipper of God will not seek *or need* an image to assist in his worship: "But the hour comes, and now is, when the true worshippers shall worship the Father *in spirit and in truth*: for the Father seeks such to worship Him. *God is a Spirit:* and they that worship Him *must worship Him in spirit and in truth*" (John 4:23-24). This is the only form of worship and praise that God accepts.

What If...?

This time, we ask: What if the whole world kept the Second Commandment? Not only would image worship disappear, but there would also be a ripple effect. The curses brought upon all humanity for breaking this law would no longer exist. Every faction of false Christianity would cease its worship of pictures and images. Virtually every other religion in this world would lose its core attraction. For example, what impact would Buddhism have on its followers without statues of Buddha? The world would move one giant step closer to the true God.

The Third Commandment— "You Shall Not Take the Name of the Lord in Vain..."

God was now ready to give the THIRD COMMANDMENT: "YOU SHALL NOT TAKE THE NAME OF THE LORD YOUR GOD IN VAIN; for the LORD will *not hold him guiltless* that takes His name in vain" (Ex. 20:7).

There is much, much more to the Third Commandment than meets the eye. When taken strictly at face value, it would seem that God is merely forbidding the speaking of His name in a careless or disrespectful manner. But there are considerably more implications within this command. They weigh heavily upon anyone who is serious about obeying the Third Commandment. When God declares, "...*for the LORD will not hold him guiltless that takes His name in vain*", we should be afraid to take this subject lightly.

The Third Commandment is tied directly to the first two. It describes the careful reverence with which God wants His name to be used at all times. The meaning of this commandment is that when people even reference the true God, they should be very careful how they do it (Psa. 111:9). They should think about the purpose—the reason—for which they mention His most holy name.

The Weight of Words

God places a great deal of importance on what we say. This is not something to be taken lightly. Christ said, in Matthew 12:36-37, "But

I say unto you, That every idle word that men shall speak, they shall give account thereof in the day of judgment. For by your words you shall be justified, and by your words you shall be condemned." And Colossians 4:6 states, "Let your speech be alway with grace, seasoned with salt." The words we speak affect others, positively or negatively, and one day we will have to answer for what we say.

Are you *prepared* for that? Perhaps a better question would be, "are you *preparing* for that?"

Words have an impact on those who hear them. The book of Proverbs contains many vital instructions concerning what we say. In chapter 17, verse 28, Solomon was inspired to write, "Even a fool, when he holds his peace, is counted wise: and he that shuts his lips is esteemed a man of understanding."

Proverbs 15:4 states, "A wholesome tongue is a tree of life: but perverseness therein is a breach in the spirit." And chapter 10 states, "The mouth of the just brings forth wisdom: but the froward tongue shall be cut out. The lips of the righteous know what is acceptable: but the mouth of the wicked speaks frowardness [perversity]" (vs. 31-32). A person's righteousness, or lack thereof, is reflected in his conversation. Christ stated in Matthew 12:34, "out of the abundance of the heart the mouth speaks."

Do your words reflect righteousness? Do you show love toward *God and neighbor* when you speak? When seeking to comply with this commandment, one must make a conscientious effort to speak words that reflect reverence toward God and genuine concern toward other people, and this includes how they are hearing you reference and honor God.

What Does It Mean?

People generally associate taking God's name in vain with obscene language. This is a correct view, but only part of the meaning. God has revealed His many names to all who carefully examine the scriptures. These names define who He is, and God expects His people to revere Him and all His attributes. When a person uses the name of God in a way that denies His true meaning and character, he is breaking the Third Commandment. In this day and age, people like to talk about God, but they are not in awe of His power or His name.

What about you? Are your words uplifting to others? Do you ever find yourself using God's name carelessly in conversation? Are you unwittingly using euphemisms, which may seem less offensive and even harmless?

A euphemism is often merely a substitute for profanity. It is, however, no less offensive, and considered just as serious, to God. Remember, we must obey God in the *spirit* of the law, and not just the *letter*. "Who also has made us able ministers of the new testament; not of the letter, but of the spirit: for the letter kills, but the spirit gives life" (II Cor. 3:6).

If a person uses euphemisms—and there are a near infinite number common today—he is merely trying to "soften the blow" of the more abrasive words that go through his mind, either consciously or subconsciously. Christ said, "But those things which proceed out of the mouth come forth from the heart [mind]; and they defile the man" (Matt. 15:18). As the saying goes, "It is the thought that counts." Our thoughts can count *for* us—or *against* us!

Are Your Words "Apples of Gold"?

A Christian follows Christ's example. I Peter 2:21 states, "For even hereunto were you called: because Christ also suffered for us, leaving us an example, that you should follow His steps."

One example that Christ left us is that of controlling His tongue. Continuing in verses 22-23: "Who did no sin, neither was guile found in His mouth: Who, when He was reviled, reviled not again; when He suffered, He threatened not; but committed Himself to Him that judges righteously."

The ultimate goal of a Christian is to become like Christ, "the Author and Finisher of our faith" (Heb. 12:2). We are exhorted to "Let this mind be in you, which was also in Christ Jesus" (Phil. 2:5).

Are you letting Christ live in you? Christ stated that a person will be known "by [his] fruits [what he *does* and *says*]" (Matt. 7:16-20). Are you learning to control your tongue?

Solomon was inspired to write, in Proverbs 25:11, "A word fitly spoken is like apples of gold in settings of silver" (NKJV). When you speak, do your words set "golden apples on a silver platter"—that is, do your words reflect careful forethought with the intent to uplift and edify others? Or do the words you use open a tomb full of poisonous asps (Rom. 3:13)?

With the many pressures we face today, it is easy to let areas such as habitual wrong use of language go un-addressed, especially if we feel such matters are not as important as others. But to God, sin is sin. We may try to "sugarcoat" foul language, but Galatians 6:7 states, "God is not mocked."

Ps. 68:4 yah!

The *Real* Importance of God's Name

In Matthew 6:7, Christ commands His followers to avoid "vain repetitions" when they pray. This is immediately followed by what is commonly known as "The Lord's Prayer." Most recite this prayer word for word, misinterpreting Christ's instructions. "In this *manner*, therefore pray," does not mean that we are to verbally copy it, word for word, every time we pray. Jesus was merely providing an overall *outline* for prayer. He was not dictating the *exact words* that we should use, nor the *exact length* of every prayer. By repeating a prayer that has been memorized (perhaps since childhood), a person actually *detracts* from the meaning and purpose of prayer, thereby literally *praying in vain*. That is serious to God!

Verse 9 tells us to "hallow" God's name. The Third Commandment instructs us to show proper respect for it. This does not mean that we should try to pronounce God's name in the original Hebrew or Greek in which it was written. Certain religious groups make a big issue of this in order to appear extremely righteous. They admit, however, that since there was no preservation of vowels in the Hebrew language, no one knows the exact pronunciation of the Hebrew word for "LORD." The real importance lies in the *meanings* that His names carry, not the way in which they are *pronounced*. (The reader will find helpful our special article "Should Christians Use 'Sacred Names'?")

God's names reveal the many aspects of His nature and character. Christians, whose hope is to one day be a part of the God Family, should honor and revere God for all that He is: our Creator, Sustainer, Healer, Provider, Lawgiver, Avenger and, ultimately, our Rewarder (Heb. 11:6; Rev. 22:12). (You may wish to read our booklet *What is Your Reward in the Next Life?* to learn more about how you can receive a future inheritance with Jesus Christ in the kingdom of God.)

King David was inspired to record, in Psalm 8:1-4, "O LORD, our Lord, how excellent is Your name in all the earth! who has set Your glory above the heavens. Out of the mouth of babes and sucklings have You ordained strength because of Your enemies, that You might still the enemy and the avenger. When I consider Your heavens, the work of Your fingers, the moon and the stars, which You have ordained; What is man, that You are mindful of him? and the son of man, that You visit him?" David, called a man after God's own heart in Acts 13:22, was in awe of God and His creation. Should we be any less in awe of Him, especially when we look around and see His handiwork, of which we are a part? We live in the Information Age, and never before has man known so much about his physical body and the world around him. "For You have possessed my reins: You have covered me in my mother's womb. I will praise You; for I am fearfully and wonderfully made: marvelous are Your works...My substance was not hid from You, when I was made in secret, and curiously wrought in the lowest parts of the earth" (Psa. 139:13-15).

Should Christians Swear?

In today's world, it is considered perfectly *normal* for people to swear and use God's name to back up their oaths! This is not only common in people's personal lives, but, with oaths, this is a standard part of most legal proceedings. But what does God's Word say about this? In Matthew 5:33-37, Christ stated, " Again, you have heard that it has been said by them of old time, You shall not forswear yourself, but shall perform unto the Lord your oaths: But I say unto you, Swear not at all; neither by heaven; for it is God's throne: nor by the earth; for it is His footstool: neither by Jerusalem; for it is the city of the great King. Neither shall you swear by your head, because you cannot make one hair white or black. But let your...yes [be], yes [and your]; no, no: for whatsoever is more than these comes of evil."

The Ninth Commandment states, "You shall not bear false witness against your neighbor" (Ex. 20:16; Deut. 5:20). Revelation 21:8 states, "...all liars, shall have their part in the lake which burns with fire and brimstone: which is the second death." The fact that this command is not binding enough in the minds of most people—even to the point that man's law *requires* the taking of oaths—is a sad commentary of how little regard people have for God's Word!

Avoiding Religious Titles

In many of the world's religions, ministers and priests assume the title of "Father" or "Reverend." What does the Bible say about this common practice?

In Matthew 23:9, Christ commanded, "...call no man your father upon the earth: for One is your Father, which is in heaven." God is our only spiritual "Father"—it is blasphemy to bestow this religious title upon any man! While it is permissible to call one's parent "father," God forbids using "Father" as a religious title.

Psalm 111:9 states, "holy and *reverend* is His name." "Reverend" means *worthy of worship*. No man is worthy of such high esteem. Paul, one of God's greatest servants, was inspired to write, "For I know that in me (that is, in my flesh) dwells no good thing: for to will is present with me; but how to perform that which is good I find not" (Rom. 7:18). Even Christ Himself stated, in Matthew 19:17, "there is none good but One, that is, God." Even Christ, who was God in the flesh (John 1:14), did not exalt Himself.

Jesus condemned the scribes and Pharisees of His day for taking to themselves the title "Rabbi" (meaning "Master")—which belongs exclusively to Christ (Matt. 23:8, 10). Anyone who dares to take to himself a title belonging to God (thereby also violating the Eighth Commandment) will one day have to REPENT before God—or suffer the consequences!

Flowing from this practice of taking to oneself the spiritual title "Father" is the tradition of "confession" to priests. Understand. Sins cannot be forgiven by any man. No human being can mediate between you and God. Jesus Christ alone holds this office. Paul wrote, "Wherefore He [Christ] is able also to save them to the uttermost that come unto God by Him, seeing He ever lives to make intercession for them" (Heb. 7:25). Paul also wrote, in I Timothy 2:5, "For there is... one Mediator between God and men, the Man Christ Jesus." Therefore, you should confess your sins to *God* only—not to another human being. Read David's example of heartfelt repentance in Psalm 51.

I John 2:1-2 states that when we sin, we have an Advocate with God the Father—Jesus Christ. When we confess our sins to God, He is faithful to forgive us. We can therefore boldly approach His throne of grace (Heb. 4:14-16).

God's Word tells us that there are, in fact, circumstances when people should confess their *faults* to others—and this is partly so that God's servants can pray for each other (Jms. 5:16). However, there is a difference between asking a brother's (or sister's) forgiveness and prayer in overcoming a human weakness or fault—and confessing past sins. A Christian should not confess his *sins* to another person, because it is only God who can *forgive* us of our sins (Mark 2:7-10; Luke 5:21-24). God also *forgets* our sins once we have repented of them, whereas people do not. (Take note: James 5:16—"Confess your faults one to another"—is the verse most often used to justify the Catholic practice of confession to priests. However, this is strictly speaking of when people have sinned against that other person. They should confess their offense to *that person*.)

Some have tried to cite John 20:23 as proof that people holding certain religious offices have the authority to forgive sins. It reads, "If you forgive the sins of any, they are forgiven them; if you retain the sins of any, they are retained" (NKJV). There is nothing here indicating that *physical* men can forgive sins in a *spiritual* sense. The context of Christ's words was about the authority that He was giving to His future apostles (John 20:21; I Cor. 5:2; I Tim. 1:20)—in this case, to disfellowship dissenters and heretics in the Church (and to later allow them back into the congregation, after repentance). (You may read our booklet *What is True Conversion?* for insight into the subject of repentance and conversion.)

In More Than Just Words

A person can take God's name in vain by more than just the words he speaks. As the saying goes, "Actions speak louder than words." Matthew 7:21 states, "'Not everyone who says unto Me, "Lord, Lord," shall enter into the kingdom of heaven; but he who does the will of My Father in heaven'" (NKJV). And in Matthew 15:8-9, when speaking to the Pharisees, who did not "practice what they preached," Christ said, "This people draws near unto Me with their mouth, and honor Me with their lips; but their heart is far from Me. But in vain they do worship Me, teaching for doctrines the commandments of men."

These are strong words!

In the end, hypocrisy is the ultimate form of taking God's name in vain. If one claims to be a Christian, but argues that "the law was nailed to the cross," then he is taking God's name in vain in the worst possible way! Christ plainly stated that He did not "come to destroy but to fulfill [the law]" (Matt. 5:17). And in Luke 6:46, He asked, "And why call you Me, Lord, Lord, and DO NOT the things which I say?"

If a person claims to be a Christian, but does not live "...by every word that proceeds out of the mouth of God" (Matt. 4:4), then he is directly breaking the Third Commandment. When someone breaks *any* of the Ten Commandments, he *automatically* breaks the Third Commandment. James 2:10 states, "For whosoever shall keep the whole law, and yet offend [stumble] in one point, he is guilty of all."

Proverbs 30:9 shows that even one who steals food when he is hungry profanes God's name: "...lest I be poor, and steal, and take the name of my God in vain."

A Christian should constantly examine himself. Paul instructed, "Examine yourselves, whether you be in the faith; prove your own selves" (II Cor. 13:5). Personal examination should include analyzing areas of your life that need improvement. Remember: taking God's name in vain can be done in actions or words. To measure spiritual growth and character development, we must analyze areas such as misusing language—expletives, euphemisms and other vain phrases that violate the Third Commandment. Realize that one can never break the habit of using foul language unless he abhors anything that can cut him off from God. All sin must be eliminated.

What If...?

We ask again: what if the whole world kept the Third Commandment? The most obvious change would be the end of profanity and the misuse of God's name. This would include all euphemisms and other vain phrases. Foul language in movies, music and television would disappear. From military drill sergeants to college football coaches, people would find new and better ways to express themselves. Even the wording of legal formalities would be rephrased.

Vain repetitions in "prayers" would stop. Also, there would be no more sermons (or "gospel" music) misusing God's name while preaching contrary to His truth. False messages about God would no longer be aired on television or radio or posted on the Internet. False Christianity and every brand of false religion would be effectively "muzzled." God's name would only be used as taught by His true servants, and with the utmost respect.

What a truly different world we have already described, and this is if just the *first three* commandments were universally observed!

The Fourth Commandment— *"Remember the Sabbath..."*

The FOURTH COMMANDMENT completes the grouping of the commandments that instruct man in his relationship with his Creator—love toward God.

Carefully read this longer command: "REMEMBER THE SABBATH DAY, TO KEEP IT HOLY. Six days shall you labor, and do all your work: but the seventh day is the Sabbath of the LORD your God: in it you shall not do any work, you, nor your son, nor your daughter, your manservant, nor your maidservant, nor your cattle, nor the stranger that is within your gates: for in six days the LORD made heaven and earth, the sea, and all that in them is, and rested the seventh day: wherefore the LORD blessed the Sabbath day, and hallowed it" (Ex. 20:8-11).

This commandment is controversial to most professing Christians. God instructs to observe it. But most simply choose to ignore it. Yet, the Fourth Commandment is the all-important *test commandment*. How we keep it demonstrates to God our willingness to honor Him and walk in His ways. God's Word describes it as a *sign* identifying the people who seek to obey God.

Long Running Debate

The subject of which day is the Christian Sabbath is one of the longest running debates about any Bible teaching. Theologians and ministers of every background and theology have offered their opinion about the "Saturday or Sunday" question.

The Fourth Commandment is the only command upon which a *covenant* was made. The two commandments that are the most lengthy and detailed—the second and the fourth—are the ones that most Christian churches have chosen to alter for their own convenience. As we saw, they "combined" the Second Commandment with the first, effectively removing it from their bibles. In regard to the Fourth Commandment, they claimed the authority to effectively change the Sabbath from the seventh day of the week to the first. We will see *why* Satan has gone to great lengths to deceive the world on the importance of the Sabbath.

The Sabbath From Creation

The book of Genesis—the name means "beginnings"—speaks almost immediately about the subject of the Sabbath—the seventh day of the week. It is as though God wanted this issue clearly established in the minds of the Bible's readers from the outset of their study of Scripture.

Near the book's beginning, immediately after the "Creation chapter" concludes, the Bible states this: "Thus the heavens and the earth were finished, and all the host of them. And on the *seventh day* God ended His work which He had made; and He RESTED on the *seventh day* from all His work which He had made. And God BLESSED the *seventh day*, and SANCTIFIED it: because that in it He had RESTED from all His work which God created and made" (Gen. 2:1-3).

While no one should have missed, or misunderstood, the weight of this passage, almost everyone has. And rather than examine it, and the many others on the subject, most merely swallow popular thinking without resistance because it is easy.

The first word in this commandment in Exodus, "remember," shows Israel *had* previously known about the Sabbath. The Ten Commandments existed and were in force before Moses (as explained in Chapter One).

God made the Sabbath as a time for man to rest from the previous six days of work. He knew that man would need this rest, physically, mentally, emotionally and spiritually. The Sabbath is a time to break away from the daily routine, commune with God, and reflect on our purpose for being.

The Sabbath begins at sunset on Friday evening and ends at sunset on Saturday evening. God blessed and sanctified *this* time, making it holy. When God confers such honor upon anything, *we should take special notice!* Many scriptures make clear why He set the Sabbath apart from the rest of the week.

Recognize that God commands man to work six days. He wants man to provide for himself (and his family) and manage his life and finances in accordance with His laws. Many verses, such as John 5:17, 36, show that both God the Father and Christ work—so should we.

Who Was the Creator?

Who was the Creator God who brought the Sabbath into being? "In the beginning was the Word, and the Word was with God, and the Word was God. The same was in the beginning with God. All things were made by Him; and without Him was not any thing made that was made" (John 1:1-3). The "Word" (Greek: *Spokesman*) was the Member of the God Family who did the creating. Verse 14 confirms the identity of the Word: Jesus Christ

"And the Word was made flesh, and dwelt among us, (and we beheld His glory, the glory as of the only begotten of the Father) full of grace and truth." This verse, and those following, point to none other than Jesus Christ. He was the One who created, sanctified (set apart) and ordained the Sabbath.

The account of the revealing of manna (bread from heaven) is closely related to the Sabbath. This occurred before Israel reached Sinai and received the law.

Before the manna was given, some important instructions for gathering it were given, in Exodus 16:4-5: "Then said the LORD unto Moses, Behold, I will rain bread from heaven for you; and the people shall go out and gather a certain rate every day, *that I may prove them, whether they will walk in My law, or no.* And it shall come to pass, that on the sixth day they shall prepare that which they bring in; and it shall be twice as much as they gather daily."

Israel was further instructed to gather only enough for each family's daily needs. Any manna left overnight would rot and breed worms. The only exception was that the double portion given on the sixth day would not deteriorate the following Sabbath morning. This miracle was intended to prove to Israel that *God would provide for their needs on the Sabbath!*

Verse 4 shows that God used the Sabbath as a test command: "…that I may PROVE them, whether they will walk in My law, or no." This was to test the Israelites' response to God's instructions. The Sabbath is also a test for God's people today.

Notice: "And it came to pass, that on the sixth day they gathered twice as much bread, two omers for one man: and all the rulers of the congregation came and told Moses. And he said unto them, This is that which the LORD has said, Tomorrow is the rest of the holy Sabbath unto the LORD: bake that which you will bake to day, and seethe [boil] that you will seethe; and that which remains over lay up for you to be kept until the morning" (Ex. 16:22-23). Besides showing that God provided extra manna on the sixth day, this also shows the preparation day was always the time to physically prepare for the Sabbath. This includes the bulk of major cooking.

Israel was told that no manna would appear on the Sabbath. They were not to gather any on that day. Yet some went out to find it anyway. God chastised Israel for this: "How long refuse you to keep My commandments and My laws? See, for that the LORD has given you the Sabbath, therefore He gives you on the sixth day the bread of two days; abide you every man in his place, let no man go out of his place [to work by gathering manna] on the seventh day. So the people rested on the seventh day" (vs. 28-30).

This account teaches an extremely important lesson. Only God controlled these factors, not Moses or any other human being. The Being who blessed and set apart the Sabbath as holy time proved that He could provide for those who observed and kept it. This event also emphasizes that the seventh day was sanctified—set apart—as the Sabbath *before* the Ten Commandments were officially given to Israel. People who keep God's commandments today will find that God will provide for *them* as well!

The Sabbath as a Covenant That Identifies

In addition to being one of the Ten Commandments, the Sabbath is so important to God that He made a special covenant (agreement or contract) with Israel for keeping it: "And the LORD spoke unto Moses, saying, Speak you also unto the children of Israel, saying, Verily My Sabbaths you shall keep: for it is a *sign* between Me and you throughout your generations; that you may know that I am the LORD that does sanctify you" (Ex. 31:12-13). Thus, the Sabbath was a *sign* identifying Israel, setting them apart for a special purpose!

Exodus 31:14-15 reveals the consequences of ignoring God's Sabbath command: "You shall keep the Sabbath therefore; for it is holy unto you: every one that defiles it shall surely be put to death: for whosoever does any work therein, that soul shall be cut off from among his people. Six days may work be done; but in the seventh is the Sabbath of rest, holy to the LORD: whosoever does any work in the Sabbath day, he shall surely be put to death."

God then presented the perpetual Sabbath covenant: "Wherefore the children of Israel shall keep the sabbath, to observe the sabbath throughout their generations, for a *perpetual covenant*. It is a *sign* between Me and the children of Israel for ever: for in six days the LORD made heaven and earth, and on the seventh day He rested, and was refreshed" (vs. 16-17).

Notice that the Sabbath command here derives its authority from the time of Creation, not from Moses.

Proof that the Sabbath is the sign between God and His true people is found in Ezekiel 20:11-13: "And I gave them My statutes, and showed them My judgments, which if a man do, he shall even live in them. Moreover also I gave them My Sabbaths, to be a sign between Me and them, that they might know that I am the LORD that sanctifies them. But the house of Israel rebelled against Me in the wilderness: they walked not in My statutes, and they despised My judgments, which if a man do, he shall even live in them; and My Sabbaths they greatly polluted."

God was so passionate about Israel's rebellion and Sabbath-breaking that He inspired Ezekiel to emphasize the seriousness of their actions: "I am the LORD your God; walk in My statutes, and keep My judgments, and do them; And hallow My Sabbaths; and they shall be a *sign between Me and you, that you may know that I am the LORD your God*. Notwithstanding the children rebelled against Me: they walked not in My statutes, neither kept My judgments to do them, which if a man do, he shall even live in them; they polluted My Sabbaths: then I said, I would pour out My fury upon them, to accomplish My anger against them in the wilderness" (vs. 19-21).

The word "sabbaths" refers to both the weekly Sabbath and the annual Holy Days, which God also describes as sabbaths. In every case above, God referred to the sabbaths as "MY" sabbaths—not

"YOUR" sabbaths or "THOSE JEWISH" sabbaths. The Sabbath belongs to God. People who reject *it* are rejecting *Him!*

No Different Today

Even today, the modern-day descendants of ancient Israel continue to rebel against God and break His sabbaths. There will come a time, after God's fury is poured out on them, that they, along with the rest of the world, will keep His sabbaths. Notice this: "As I live, says the Lord God, surely with a mighty hand, and with a stretched out arm, and with fury poured out, will I rule over you: and I will bring you out from the people, and will gather you out of the countries wherein you are scattered, with a mighty hand, and with a stretched out arm, and with fury poured out" (Ezek. 20:33-34).

These verses depict the arrival of the now soon-coming Millennium, when Jesus Christ and the saints will rule in righteousness and equity. He will gather the Israelite survivors of the Great Tribulation and the Day of the Lord and bring them back to the land He has reserved for them. This time, Israel will obey. (Read our booklet *Revelation Explained at Last!*)

The following scriptures should help you appreciate the unique opportunity that Israel was given by God. Psalms 147:19-20 reads, "He shows His word unto Jacob, His statutes and His judgments unto Israel. He has not dealt so with any nation: and as for His judgments, they have not known them." Now notice Amos 3:1-2: "Hear this word that the Lord has Spoken against you, O children of Israel, against the whole family which I brought up from the land of Egypt, saying, You only have I known of all the families of the earth: therefore I will punish you for all your iniquities."

Throughout Israel's history, both the northern ten-tribe nation of Israel ("the house of Israel" or Northern Kingdom), and Judah ("the house of Judah" or Southern Kingdom) have been guilty of breaking the Sabbath. The house of Israel abandoned the Sabbath and most of God's other laws. As a result, these tribes went into captivity for many centuries, lost their identity, and became lost to history. The nation of Judah also went into captivity because of Sabbath-breaking and idolatry. Jewish leaders such as Ezra and Nehemiah, who returned after their captivity, were diligent in keeping the Sabbath. They realized that neglecting this vital command was the main reason for their captivity (Neh. 13:17-18). Turning away from observing the Sabbath always leads to idolatry and worshipping false gods. Sabbath-keeping shows God the course one has chosen to follow.

(My vitally important book, *America and Britain in Prophecy*, carefully explains why Israel was taken into captivity, and what the twin sins of Sabbath-breaking and idolatry mean for these nations today. This book is not to be missed.)

Christ's Teaching and Example

Christ made a profound statement during a confrontation with the Pharisees. It is never spoken of in countless thousands of churches and Sunday schools: "And He said unto them, *The Sabbath was made for man* [not "the Jews"], and not man for the Sabbath: Therefore THE SON OF MAN IS LORD ALSO OF THE SABBATH" (Mark 2:27-28). *Read*

Jesus stressed that the Sabbath was made *for man* and *his needs*—to rest, be refreshed and mainly to commune with God. Yet the Pharisees acted as if human beings were created to comply with their endless rules. They had become lost in a maze of regulations, which separated them from the Sabbath's true meaning. Christ said that the Sabbath was *made for man*. Notice, He said this day of rest was made for man—*all humanity*—not just for the Jews. He explained that He was Lord of the Sabbath (vs. 28). As Maker, Sustainer and Author of the Sabbath Covenant, Christ alone deserves the title "Lord of the Sabbath."

Jesus showed that the Pharisees' condemnation of gathering corn to be eaten on the Sabbath was unfounded (vs. 23-26). His example demonstrated that it was permissible to gather food on the Sabbath to fulfill immediate hunger.

In Mark 3:1-6, the Pharisees closely watched Christ to see whether He would, on the Sabbath, heal a man who had a withered hand. When Christ perceived that they sought to accuse Him, He responded, "Is it lawful to do good on the Sabbath days, or to do evil? to save life, or to kill?" (vs. 4). The Pharisees would not answer Him. Christ immediately healed the man, after which the Pharisees sought to kill Him. What an indictment against self-righteous human nature!

Christ's example reveals that it is permissible to do good on the Sabbath and to relieve suffering. This is in harmony with the spirit of the Fourth Commandment.

In the same account found in Matthew 12:11-12, Christ used the analogy of rescuing an animal in distress, with which the Pharisees agreed. Yet, they did not allow for Christ to heal a suffering human being on the Sabbath. He used a similar analogy in Luke 13:15-17, of loosing livestock from a stall to lead them away for watering on the Sabbath, with which the Pharisees also agreed. But they protested Christ's healing of an Israelite woman bound with an affliction for 18 years. This account also confirms that Christ allowed certain *necessary* physical duties to be carried out on the Sabbath, such as feeding and watering livestock. However, this is *not* license to plan or do non-emergency work on the Sabbath!

The Sabbath is made for mankind. Instead of being a time of strict "do's and don'ts," it can be a time to do good and relieve suffering, as well as a time of rest and worship.

Like many of the Bible's teachings, proper, correct Sabbath-keeping has become a controversial issue. Is the Sabbath governed by a strict list of "do's and don'ts"? Christ said that the Sabbath was made for man. In theory, if men made the Sabbath, they would have the right to tell you how to keep it. But since it was made *for* man, not *by* man, man does not determine how it should be kept. God does! What does this mean? You can know how to properly keep and enjoy the Sabbath—as God intended!

God gave man His laws so that we can enjoy life to the fullest. Contrary to what many believe, those laws are not a burden. They were given so that we can have a proper relationship with God and our fellowman. Jesus also taught, "The thief comes not, but for to steal, and to kill, and to destroy: I am come that they might have life, and that they might have it more abundantly" (John 10:10).

Most professing Christians "agree" with nine of the Ten Commandments. They still at least vaguely understand that it is wrong to worship other gods and practice idolatry, although they unwittingly do so. Most would say that it is wrong to take God's name in vain. Some feel that it is at least a good idea to show some degree of respect to parents. Some are of the opinion that it is morally wrong to kill, steal, lie, commit adultery, and covet the things of others.

It is entirely another matter, however, that very few people actively attempt to *practice* these nine commandments as a way of life. After all, they just *know* that the law was "done away." Nevertheless, they still basically accept them as "nice principles."

But when it comes to God's command to "Remember the Sabbath Day, to keep it holy" (Exod. 20:8; Lev. 23:3; Deut. 5:12), even those who desire to keep it simply do not know how.

Sabbath Convocation

Leviticus 23 covers the subject of the seven annual sabbaths, or Holy Days. Verses 1-3 explain the weekly Sabbath. Notice: "And the LORD spoke unto Moses, saying, Speak unto the children of Israel, and say unto them, Concerning the feasts of the LORD, which you shall proclaim to be holy convocations, even these are My feasts. Six days shall work be done: but the seventh day is the Sabbath of rest, an holy convocation; you shall do no work therein: it is the Sabbath of the LORD in all your dwellings."

The weekly Sabbath is a holy convocation—a commanded assembly, during which God's people are given spiritual food from His servants. The Sabbath service is a delight and joy, and has always been eagerly anticipated by God's people through the ages. Notice the admonition given in Hebrews 10:24-25: "And let us consider one another to provoke unto love and to good works: Not forsaking the assembling of ourselves together, as the manner of some is; but exhorting one another: and so much the more, as you see the day approaching." It is crucial that God's people assemble each week to receive His spiritual food, as well as for fellowship.

The book of Isaiah contains inspiring and reassuring encouragement for those who do not pollute God's Sabbath and diligently follow His Law:

"Neither let the son of the stranger, that has joined himself to the LORD, speak, saying, The LORD has utterly separated me from His people: neither let the eunuch say, Behold, I am a dry tree. For thus says the LORD unto the eunuchs *that keep My Sabbaths*, and choose the things that please Me, and take hold of My covenant; even unto them will I give in Mine house and within My walls a place and a name better than of sons and of daughters: I will give them an everlasting name, that shall not be cut off" (56:3-5).

But Only With the Living, Active One True Church

We have seen that assembling together in spirit and in truth to learn is part of God's requirement, but what else does God require one to do in order to properly observe His day?

The subject of the Sabbath is inseparable from that of the identity and location of the true Church, introduced earlier. Of course, many groups claim to be God's true Church. Some of these observe the Sabbath to one degree or another, or in one form or another. Yet, in every case, all "Sabbath-keeping churches"—there are no exceptions—teach a great many false doctrines.

When individuals first learn about the Sabbath, they often believe that they can assemble with *any* Sabbath-keeping organization or group. But just because a church meets on the true Sabbath does not mean it is the TRUE Church of God.

Jesus said that He would build "His Church" (Matt. 16:18). He called it "a building" that is "fitly framed together" (Eph. 2:21), and built with Himself as the foundation. Jesus Christ is literally "building a building" consisting of brethren whom He calls "lively [living] stones" (1 Pet. 2:5). Psalm 127:1 declares, "Except the Lord build the house, they labor in vain that build it."

Christ is continuing to build His Church today, and you have come in contact with it!

Lives are changing every day due to the Work of God, the Work that Christ is doing through His human instruments in HIS Church.

God commands you to assemble with the Body of Christ—a single, unified organization of Spirit-begotten sons of God! There is only ONE such group. Just any organization will not suffice—no matter what men may say! To those who are unsure about which "Church of God" to attend, do not misunderstand! You cannot please God *and* assemble with those who compromise God's truth. That does not please God! Read 2 John 7-10, Titus 3:9-11 and Romans 16:17.

You are urged to carefully study my thorough and fascinating book *The History of the True Church – Where Is It Today?*

The Sabbath—a Delight

Another passage in Isaiah provides some guidelines as to how to keep the Sabbath: "If you turn away your foot from the Sabbath, from doing *your pleasure* on My holy day; and *call the Sabbath a delight*, the holy of the LORD, honorable; and shall honor Him, not doing your own ways, nor finding your own pleasure, nor speaking your own words: Then shall you delight yourself in the LORD; and I will cause you to ride upon the high places of the earth, and feed you with the heritage of Jacob your father: for the mouth of the LORD has spoken it" (58:13-14).

The term "turn away your foot from the Sabbath" means that you should not walk over the Sabbath, or forget that it is holy time set aside by the Creator. "Not doing your pleasure" refers to misusing the Sabbath for hobbies, sports activities, or other personal pursuits.

There *are* certain activities that are beneficial in helping the observant appreciate the Sabbath and God's creation. These could include taking a short, refreshing walk or perhaps playing uplifting or relaxing music on the piano. Since it is a time of rest, you should avoid certain activities, such as running or exercising.

Remember, the Sabbath is a feast day, so a special Sabbath meal would be appropriate. When we understand and keep the Sabbath as God intended, it will indeed be a *delight*. (For more information about the Sabbath, and to see how counterfeit Christianity changed the seventh-day Sabbath to the first day of the week, read our comprehensive book *Saturday or Sunday – Which is the Sabbath?* There is no more clear and thorough book you could read on the subject.)

The promise attached to the Sabbath command is significant. To "ride upon the high places of the earth" means to be elevated and promoted by blessings that only God can provide. This could include better health, a more rewarding job, wisdom and understanding, or other blessings. God is not bribing anyone into keeping the Sabbath. The real rewards He wants us to seek are the spiritual ones.

What If...?

What if the whole world obeyed the Fourth Commandment? What if every nation suspended all activities for 24 hours each week? All people would grow personally close to God as a result of obeying Him. If the entire world kept the Sabbath and Holy Days, everyone would know who the true God is because the Sabbath identifies Him and His people.

Keeping the Sabbath would most likely lead to keeping the other laws of God. Using the Sabbath for the purposes He intended would focus people's minds on His way. This would leave this world's false religions in shambles, because God's laws would then replace their own laws, twisted reasonings and false interpretations. This is why Satan has gone to such great lengths to blind the world from the benefits of keeping the Fourth Commandment.

Words Most Plain!

These commandments are not difficult to understand. The God of the Bible speaks plainly—He says what He means and means what He says! (Note that God repeats for emphasis in Deuteronomy 5 the same Ten Commandments verbatim.)

We might pause at this point again and ask: Do these first four commands, when understood collectively, sound like the laws of a God who takes lightly those who worship any other but Himself? Do they seem like mere wishful instruction on the part of this God—things that He only *hopes* His followers will remember to do? Do they sound like the words of a God who is willing to let people worship idols, false gods or even any other wrong *form* of supposedly who and what He is, as long as the proponent proclaims such to be the true God? Do they reflect a God who does not care which day you select to worship Him as long as you pick one?

It has been said that the first four commandments describe how to love God and the last six reveal how to love one's fellow man. Put another way, the first four commandments explain how to establish a *relationship* with the true God and the last six how to build relationships with human beings.

A relationship with the God of the Bible begins with a recognition, understanding and acceptance of the first four commandments. All other approaches will preclude contact with the true God!

The Fifth Commandment— "Honor Your Father and Mother..."

The Fifth Commandment is the first that deals with man's relation with his fellow man—love toward neighbor, in this case, parents. Exodus 20:12 reads, "HONOR YOUR FATHER AND YOUR MOTHER: that your days may be long upon the land which the Lord your God gives you."

This commandment *connects* the first four commandments, "love toward God" with the last five, "love toward neighbor." This is because honoring God bears a strong relationship to honoring parents. The implications of this commandment are serious.

Since a child learns to honor his parents before learning to honor God, this is the natural transition *from* love toward neighbor *to* love toward God and vice versa.

This commandment is directed to children, *regardless of age*. Notice that God promises long life to all those who obey this pivotal commandment.

The concept of *honor* begins with the concept of *obedience*. In life, there are many things that a child must learn to respect. There are boundaries of acceptable conduct that have to be ingrained. Once the value and benefits of obedience are ingrained, children have a jumpstart in the right direction.

It is important to always remember that discipline, tempered with love, not only defines the boundaries, but also instills confidence and security within a child. He knows that his parents always have his best interests in mind. Although most children will not admit it, they prefer rules and standards that define the set limits of what is permissible and what is not.

The Fifth Commandment Ignored

Everything that leads to fulfillment in life is summed up in the Ten Commandments. The value of teaching a young child these laws is absolutely priceless. In these perilous times, immediate and extended families are not as tightly knit as they once were. The influence of diligent parents overseeing their children's daily needs, both physical *and* spiritual, has largely become a thing of the past.

By the 1960s in much of the Western world, the daily pressures of life boiled over in various college campuses. These revolts were compounded by new influences that dropped morals to lower depths, such as illegal drug use (marijuana, LSD, heroin, etc.). Others included the hippie movement, unprecedented promiscuity, chaotic hard rock music, and the "counterculture" that opposed the values of "the establishment" and promoted anarchy. In effect, this counterculture mentality pressured youth to essentially disown the principles of the Fifth Commandment, or face rejection by their peers. To be part of the "in" crowd, youth were expected to sever close parental ties, and embrace their peers' values. Most adults then were shocked at the open rebellion of youth. Nothing of this kind had ever happened before and they were convinced that things could not grow any worse. But they have grown worse—much worse!

Today, some even call their parents or their mates' parents by first name, dishonoring the high office of a parent.

These influences have not dissipated. They became ingrained in the minds of the children and grandchildren of the counterculture movement.

Many people of this third generation suffer from deep-seated problems resulting from long-term effects of their parents' and grandparents' mistakes. Many were born illegitimate, as were their parents.

Earlier generations could at least look back to their grandparents and see examples of moral, and even a certain "religious," discipline, hard work, and endurance in adversity. Recent generations have been denied such anchors of stability. Materialism and the downward spiral of morality have warped vast numbers of youth—sometimes beyond redemption. It is common to find children repeatedly sent to detention programs due to deeply imbedded criminal behavior. In recent years, school shooting massacres have become almost commonplace. Public counselors are swamped with youth behavioral cases, accompanied by new upsurges in drug and alcohol abuse. Law enforcement has uncovered numerous bombing plots engineered by students.

Many ask, "Where did we go wrong?" The next step is usually to blame television, music, movies and the other usual "suspects"— schools, bad neighbors, poverty, environment, etc. While these issues are definitely part of the problem, the bigger picture must be considered. When a civilization cut off from God becomes more and more materialistic, moral collapse is predictable and unstoppable.

The Vital Role of Parenthood

God intended that families consist of a father and mother who diligently apply His ways in childrearing. The *family* is the basic unit— not a "village," as advocated by today's liberals. The presence of *both* parents is vital to doing the job correctly. The absence of either parent results in a crippled family structure. In the eyes of a child, both parents represent God, in that they provide for the child's needs similar to the way that God provides for the needs of adults. A child's relationship with his parents during his formative years determines how his relationship will be with God.

The New Testament admonishes parents to avoid either extreme of being too lenient or too harsh. Notice: "Children, obey your parents in all things: for this is well pleasing unto the Lord. Fathers, provoke not your children to anger, lest they be discouraged" (Col. 3:20-21). A parent who establishes firm guidelines and administers prompt discipline gets better results than one who withholds discipline, resorting to constant fussing and nagging. This type of "correction" only results in loss of respect from the child. Since God expects parents to represent Him, they are obligated to follow His rules and examples in disciplining and training.

Notice Ephesians 6:1-4: "Children, obey your parents in the Lord: for this is right. Honor your father and mother; (which is the first commandment with promise) that it may be well with you, and you may live long on the earth. And, you fathers, provoke not your children to wrath: but bring them up in the nurture and admonition of the Lord."

This key scripture stresses and builds directly upon the Fifth Commandment. Paul stresses its importance, noting that it is the first commandment with promise—long life. If children are taught to properly fear and honor their parents, they will fear and honor *God* as they reach adulthood. God's principles are guaranteed to work. As our Creator, He understands the human mind. Long life is virtually assured for anyone who obeys this commandment.

Deuteronomy 6:6-9 is a vital scripture that is often forgotten in child rearing: "And these words [the Ten Commandments, along with the statutes and precepts], which I command you this day, shall be in your heart: and you shall teach them diligently unto your children, and shall talk of them when you sit in your house, and when you walk by the way, and when you lie down, and when you rise up. And you shall bind them for a sign upon your hand, and they shall be as frontlets between your eyes. And you shall write them upon the posts of your house, and on your gates."

If you are a parent, strongly consider taking the time to read our most helpful and inspiring book *Train Your Children God's Way!*

From the Book of Proverbs

Notice some of the Proverbs pertaining to childtraining, instruction and correction:

"My son, despise not the chastening of the LORD; neither be weary of His correction: For whom the LORD loves He corrects; even as a father the son in whom he delights" (3:11-12).

"He that spares his rod hates his son: but he that loves him chastens him betimes [early or promptly]" (13:24).

"Chasten your son while there is hope, and let not your soul spare for his crying" (19:18).

"When the scorner is punished, the simple is made wise: and when the wise is instructed, he receives knowledge" (21:11).

"Train up a child in the way he should go: and when he is old, he will not depart from it" (22:6).

Also read these other Proverbs: 22:15; 23:13-14; 25:12; 28:23; 29:15, 17.

The Fifth Commandment in Perspective

After giving the Ten Commandments, God's initial instructions to Moses show how seriously He regarded complete obedience to His law. Notice this warning: "And he that SMITES his father, or his mother, shall be surely PUT TO DEATH…And he that CURSES his father, or his mother, shall surely be PUT TO DEATH" (Ex. 21:15, 17). Strong words— and Leviticus 20:9 repeats this.

God knows that anyone who dishonors others, especially parents, will also dishonor Him. Many people today notice these judgments and conclude, "That God of the Old Testament was harsh!" This totally misses the point. Instead, they should ask, "Do I regard God's living law with the due fear that God required of physical Israel?"

Since Ephesians 6:1 teaches, "Children, obey your parents in the Lord: for this is right," parents must diligently conduct themselves in ways that deserve honor from their children. They must lead by example.

The phrase "in the Lord" defines the *conditions* of obedience. This term emphasizes that obedience to God comes *before* obedience to parents. For example, if a parent tells his child to mow the lawn on the Sabbath, the child must put God's Law *first*, even if it means disobeying his parents. "In the Lord" means that any parental command that is against God's laws would have to be *respectfully* declined.

Mark 7:9-13 reads, "And He said unto them, Full well you reject the commandment of God, that you may keep your own tradition. For Moses said, Honor your father and your mother; and, Whoso curses father or mother, let him die the death: but you say, If a man shall say to his father or mother, it is Corban [a consecrated or dedicated offering], that is to say, a gift, by whatsoever you might be profited by me; he shall be free. And you suffer him no more to do ought for his father or his mother; making the word of God of none effect through your tradition, which you have delivered: and many such like things do you."

The scribes and Pharisees got around the spirit of the law by legitimizing their neglect of their elderly parents. They did this to increase their offerings for the sake of political clout. Christ condemned their hypocrisy. He defined the obligation to give financial and other assistance to one's elderly parents.

This is further explained by Paul in I Timothy 5:16. Notice: "If any man or woman that believes have widows, *let them relieve them, and let not the Church be charged*; that it may relieve them that are widows indeed."

Members of God's Church are taught to help support their own elderly parents (widows in this case), so that the Church would be relieved of that burden. The Fifth Commandment demands that we honor and support our parents until the end of their lives.

What If...?

We face a similar question to previous commands: what if the whole world obeyed the Fifth Commandment? The end of juvenile delinquency would only be the beginning. Honoring parents would naturally lead to honoring God.

Reform schools and youth detention centers would close or would become educational centers. Drug dealers and gangs would be out of business—as youths would honor and obey their parents who warned them about these dangers. Without drug habits to feed, theft would decrease.

Children could safely walk to school without worrying about gangland drive-by shootings. With more diligent parental guidance, we would see positive changes in the media and in the values that they project. Respect for the elderly would reappear, along with respect for authority, including police officers and teachers. Generations would live longer as they would receive the promised blessing due to showing honor to their parents.

The Sixth Commandment— "You Shall Not Kill"

The SIXTH COMMANDMENT is recorded in Exodus 20:13: "YOU SHALL NOT KILL." The Hebrew word for "kill" is *ratsach*, but "murder" is a more accurate translation. This term means a willful, deliberate and malicious act, as opposed to an action resulting in accidental death. (God does not view accidental death between parties as murder – see Deuteronomy 19:1-13).

In a world cut off from God, many today have little regard for the sanctity of human life. God said, "He that smites a man, so that he die, shall be surely put to death" (Ex. 21:12).

In most Western societies today, committing murder could cost the murderer as little as five years in prison, with probation!

Since God is the Giver of life, He forbids man from taking it. This includes *suicide* and *abortion*. Mankind is made in the image and likeness of God and has been given a mind and potential destiny to be born into God's Family. This is why we must respect human life with the sanctity that God intended.

Neverending Wars

The horror of war has wracked the world for thousands of years. Its fruits are terror, destruction, economic upheaval, orphaned children, population displacement, widespread devastation of the land, atrocities, hunger, disease, untold suffering, misery, despair, injuries, death and even genocide. All of this yields *greater* hatred and revenge, endless retaliation and more war, because nothing is ever permanently resolved through military conflict.

Ever since Cain slew Abel (Gen. 4), human history has been a chronicle of killing and war. What began as family or tribal disagreements later developed into conflicts between nations. The conflict between Cain and Abel was motivated by jealousy and contempt, and so have been the agendas of nations throughout history.

Additionally, long-standing ethnic, tribal and religious differences, coupled with boundary disputes and outright aggression to seize the land or property of others, have always served to fuel the next war fought between the same peoples or nations.

War has affected all nations in every period of history. Many nations have made war their primary means of livelihood—not just a means of defense or protection. Those nations that chose not to actively pursue war had to at least expend much time, money and effort to protect themselves—sometimes having to "buy" peace by paying tribute to powers that could have dominated them.

In the mid-1960s, a Norwegian statistician programmed a computer to count all of the wars through the 6,000 years of mankind's history. It concluded that 14,531 wars had been fought. But this was merely the number that were *known* and *recorded*. How many more were not? And consider that this was several decades ago. Countless more have been fought since then. Of course, this does not count the endless stream of individual terrorist acts, such as suicide bombings and other assaults, which occur in undeclared wars.

Incredible new weapons technology has forever altered the face of war. "Smart" bombs, which are laser-guided to bring precision and efficiency to the art of killing, have replaced many types of "dumb" bombs. Military scientists have now developed cluster bombs, called "daisy cutters" because they cut down large numbers of human beings, like a lawnmower cuts grass. Also, there are newer bombs called "bunker-busters" that can penetrate deep into the earth in pursuit of enemies hiding in caves before detonating and killing the inhabitants.

Various highly lethal kinds of attack aircraft now exist—helicopters, jets, bombers, gunships—that have brought conventional warfare to a pinnacle of destructive capability never before known. A 2,000 pound, precision, satellite-guided bomb has a "kill zone" of 1,300 yards radius (almost three quarters of a mile). It kills and maims indiscriminately. So this can sometimes involve "friendly fire" casualties, in which one's own troops are hit.

Modern military thinkers and strategists are now forced to think and talk in terms of protection from, or delivery of, "weapons of mass destruction." The killing capability of nuclear, chemical and biological weapons and, now, radiological or "dirty bombs," is almost indescribably horrible.

But this presents no problem because men have devised ways to justify whatever they do. The greatest of all social problems, *war*, is no exception! And man's pattern of not asking God what He thinks is also no exception. When nations have *already decided* that it is in their best interest to go to war, all that remains is the task of spelling out the human rationale to justify what they have *pre-determined* to do. Enter the moralists, ethicists, philosophers, politicians and religionists.

But God thunders to all peoples of every nation, "You shall not kill"! (The serious reader will wish to read our booklet *War, Killing and the Military*.)

Christians and the Sixth Commandment

Christians are those who follow—who copy—Jesus Christ (I Peter 2:21; Phil. 2:5). We must ask, "What would He do if He were here today?" Would Christ bear arms and kill His fellow man? Did He teach contrary to the Ten Commandments? Did Paul and John merely record their *own opinions* about "love," the law and sin? What did Christ actually teach about fighting, hating and killing?

Jesus was foretold in Isaiah to come and "magnify the law" (42:21). Is there evidence that He did this?

Matthew 5:21-22 states, "*You have heard* that it was said by them of old time, YOU SHALL NOT KILL; and whosoever shall kill shall be in danger of the judgment: *But I say* unto you, That *whosoever is angry* with his brother *without a cause* shall be in danger of the judgment: and whosoever shall say to his brother, Raca, shall be in danger of the council: but whosoever shall say, You fool, shall be in danger of hell fire."

This is serious instruction! It obviously *does* expand—magnify—the Sixth Commandment.

Verses 38-39 and 43-44 contain more: "You have heard that it has been said, *An eye for an eye, and a tooth for a tooth:* but I say unto you, that you resist not evil: but whosoever shall smite you on your right cheek, turn to him the other also…You have heard that it has been said, *You shall love your neighbor, and hate your enemy.* But I say unto you, LOVE YOUR ENEMIES, *bless* them that curse you, *do good* to them that hate you, and *pray for* them which despitefully use you, and persecute you."

Three times Christ said, "You have heard," followed by, "But I say." Each time, He made the law even *more binding.* Those who claim to seek God will be unable to explain away the truth of these verses.

How important are these things to God? Verse 45 answers: "That you may be the children of your Father…in heaven." Just like any human parent, God expects His children to obey Him. Christ's command is so important that it qualifies whom God considers to be His children.

Notice what is at stake for those who ignore and disobey God: "We know that we have passed from death unto life, because we love the brethren. He that loves not his brother *abides in death.* WHOSOEVER HATES HIS BROTHER IS A MURDERER: and you know that *no murderer has eternal life* abiding in him" (I John 3:14-15).

Again, this is a most serious instruction! Ultimately, all violence and aggression come from hate and anger. Christ was very specific about the need to control these attitudes—and what would result if one did not. To merely "love not" another leads to eternal death.

God gives His Spirit to those who obey Him—who have repented of sin. Notice the following account involving John the Baptist: "Then came also publicans to be baptized, and said unto him, Master, what shall we do?…and the soldiers likewise demanded of him, saying, And what shall we do? And he said unto them, *Do violence to no man*, neither accuse any falsely; and be content with your wages" (Luke 3:12, 14).

The Old Testament God who thundered from Mount Sinai, "You shall not kill," is the same God—Jesus Christ!—who thunders the identical command to you and me today. He further commands, "Do violence to no man."

As a wise instructor once observed, "Christ is pictured as a rebellious young man who came to do away with His Father's law." Yet, the opposite is true.

Here is one more proof that Jesus Christ was the God of the Old Testament. Paul wrote, "And [Israel] did all drink the same spiritual drink: for they drank of that spiritual ROCK that followed them: *and that Rock was Christ*" (I Cor. 10:4). Theologians and religionists try to place Christ in conflict with—in opposition to—the God of the Old Testament. How absurd!

When David referred to God as "my Rock," he meant the New Testament Jesus Christ. Moses was given the Ten Commandments by Christ, and Abraham talked with Him face-to-face (Ex. 3:14; John 8:58).

From the Book of Proverbs

There are many proverbs on the subject of anger, strife and hate, and they become their own vital, longer Bible study. Anger is not condemned as a sin, but is a frame of mind that can easily lead to sin if allowed to fester. There are passages that explain anger might, on relatively rare occasion, have a place. Ephesians 4:26 states, "Be you angry, and sin not: let not the sun go down upon your wrath."

The following proverbs explain the dangers of harboring anger and wrath:

"He that is void of wisdom despises his neighbor: but a man of understanding holds his peace" (11:12).

"A fool's wrath is presently known: but a prudent man covers shame" (12:16).

"He that is soon angry deals foolishly: and a man of wicked devices is hated" (14:17).

"He that is slow to wrath is of great understanding: but he that is hasty of spirit exalts folly" (14:29).

Also read Proverbs 15:18; 16:32; 17:14, 19; 18:19; 19:11, 19; 20:3, 22; 22:10, 24-25; 25:8, 28; 29:10, 22.

Excuses People Make

Human beings are wonderfully skilled at justifying their actions, including all manner of breaking the Sixth Commandment. Many point to Israel's destruction of most of the nations of Canaan as an excuse to kill. But *why* did God command Israel to destroy the Canaanites?

Notice this: "When the LORD your God shall bring you into the land where you go to possess it, and has cast out many nations before you, the Hittites, and the Girgashites, and the Amorites, and the Canaanites, and the Perizzites, and the Hivites, and the Jebusites, seven nations greater and mightier than you; and when the LORD your God shall deliver them before you; you shall smite them, and utterly destroy them; you shall make no covenant with them, nor show mercy unto them: neither shall you make marriages with them; your daughter you shall not give unto his son, nor his daughter shall you take unto your son. For they will turn away your son from following Me, that they may serve other gods: so will the anger of the Lord be kindled against you, and destroy you suddenly. But thus shall you deal with them; you shall destroy their altars, and break down their images, and cut down their groves, and burn their graven images with fire" (Deut. 7:1-5).

The reasons become clear why God was forced to destroy these nations instead of allowing them to co-exist with Israel.

God, as the Giver of life, has the right to decide who lives or who dies. He decided to destroy the Canaanites because of their immorality and corruption, which included child sacrifice, rank idolatry and gross perversion. Modern nations are in danger of receiving the same death penalty.

God knew that this was inevitable and told Abram, over 400 years before, "And you shall go to your fathers in peace; you shall be buried in a good old age. But in the fourth generation they [Abram's seed—the nation Israel] shall come here again: for the iniquity of the Amorites is not yet full" (Gen. 15:15-16).

Another excuse used to justify violence and killing is the "obligation" of vengeance. Romans 12:19 states, "Dearly beloved, avenge not yourselves, but rather give place unto wrath: for it is written, Vengeance is Mine; I will repay, says the Lord."

This verse shows that vengeance cannot be used as an excuse for violence. Living by this scripture would eliminate useless, agonizing worry and suffering! It is better to let God settle the score.

Leviticus 19:18 states, "You shall not avenge, nor bear any grudge against the children of your people, but you shall love your neighbor as yourself: I am the Lord."

Make no mistake. Men and nations are not free to go to war and kill because of any supposed Old Testament authority to do so.

Media's Devastating Influence

Of all the factors that influence youth, hardly any dominates more than television. Its effect has been nothing less than devastating. Consider the following quotes.

"American children watch an average of three to four hours of television daily. Television can be a powerful influence in developing value systems and shaping behavior. Unfortunately, much of today's television programming is violent. Hundreds of studies of the effects of TV violence on children and teenagers have found that children may: (1) become "immune" to the horror of violence, (2) gradually accept violence as a way to solve problems, (3) imitate the violence they observe on television, and (4) identify with characters, victims and/or victimizers...

"Extensive viewing of television violence by children causes greater aggressiveness. Sometimes, watching a single violent program can increase aggressiveness. Children who view shows in which violence is very realistic, frequently repeated or unpunished, are more likely to imitate what they see. Children with emotional, behavioral, learning or impulse control problems may be more easily influenced by TV violence. The impact of TV violence may be immediately evident in the child's behavior or may surface years later, and young people can even be affected when the family atmosphere shows no tendency toward violence" (*American Academy of Child & Adolescent Psychiatry*, "Children and TV Violence," No. 13, April 1999).

"Do you despair at the sight of the youngster in a trance in front of the television set? You are not alone. With sets turned on in the inner city for 11 hours a day, with video, pay per view and multiplying cable channels, TV has become the closest and most constant companion for American children. It has become the nation's mom and pop, storyteller, baby sitter, preacher and teacher. Our children watch an astonishing 5,000 hours by the first grade and 19,000 hours by the end of high school—more time than they spend in class...

"The concern is that in later life, those conditioned to violence will intuitively continue to regard it as exciting, charismatic and effective. Consider how pervasive it is. By the age of 18, according to one estimate, a youngster will have seen 200,000 acts of violence on TV, including 40,000 murders. TV Guide looked at 10 channels on one normal 18-hour day and found 1,846 individual acts of violence—and every hour of prime time carries six to eight acts of violence. Violence has become normal, the Pied Piper to lure the vulnerable to a darker world.

"The youthful world has become dramatically more violent. Consider this piece of anecdotal evidence turned up by CBS News: The seven top problems in public schools in 1940 were identified by teachers as talking out of turn, chewing gum, making noise, running in the halls, cutting in line, dress-code infractions and littering. By

1980, the seven top problems had been identified as suicide, assault, robbery, rape, drug abuse, alcohol abuse and pregnancy" (*U.S. News & World Report*, "The Victims of TV Violence," Aug. 2, 1993, Vol. 115, Issue 5, p. 64)

"In World War II, the Japanese would make some of their young, unblooded soldiers bayonet innocent prisoners to death. Their friends would cheer them on. Afterwards, all these soldiers were treated to the best meal they had had in months, sake, and the 'comfort girls.' The result? They learned to associate violence with pleasure.

"This technique is so morally reprehensible that there are very few examples of it in modern U.S. military training. But the media is doing it to our children. Kids watch vivid images of human death and suffering, and they learn to associate it with laughter, cheers, popcorn, soda and their girlfriend's perfume.

"After the Jonesboro shootings, one of the high school teachers told me about her students' reaction when she told them that someone had shot a bunch of their little brothers, sisters, and cousins in the middle school. 'They laughed,' she told me with dismay, 'They laughed.' We have raised a generation of barbarians who have learned to associate human death and suffering with pleasure" (*National Forum*, "Teaching Kids to Kill," Fall 2000, Vol. 80, Issue 4, p. 10).

It is not an exaggeration to say that television has now *replaced God*, that Hollywood has replaced as teachers the Levitical Priesthood, and a cheap, shallow world of fantasy has replaced the truth of the Bible, virtually the world over!

What If...?

Once again, we present the same question: what if the whole world kept the Sixth Commandment, even just in the letter of the law? Military assaults and invasions would no longer be carried out. The ever-present threats of nuclear, chemical, and biological warfare would no longer exist. The defense budgets of all nations would be available for more constructive uses.

On the domestic level, people would no longer have to live in constant fear for their lives. Homicides, suicides and abortions would end. Police forces would be reduced. Television and movies would not glorify violence and murder. This is another glimpse into Jesus Christ's soon-coming millennial rule, where individuals and nations will finally be at peace.

The Seventh Commandment—
"You Shall Not
Commit Adultery"

The SEVENTH COMMANDMENT is found in Exodus 20:14: "YOU SHALL NOT COMMIT ADULTERY."

This commandment was given to protect the honor and sanctity of marriage and, like the Fifth Commandment, it also protects the entire family unit.

Before we can understand all that God teaches about the true purposes of sex and marriage—and why the seventh command—we must examine what is occurring today.

Sex-drenched Society

The world is now drenched—actually drowning—in a deluge of sex, with much or most of it having no connection to any real meaning or right purpose. More than ever in history, all mankind is awash in every conceivable kind of sexual pleasure, fantasy, perversion and pursuit—in or out of marriage, and with fewer and fewer people any longer making a distinction between the two. There has come to be no end to—and virtually no limits on—advertisements, television programs, movies, books, magazines, articles, photographs and web-sites for every kind of pornography and sex-related activity that the misguided creative genius of human beings could devise.

The sexual revolution of the latter twentieth century changed the entire world—and not for the better. During this period, the idea of "sex without boundaries" did, in fact, escalate beyond all bounds. The advent of cable television, the Internet and the vast expanse of every conceivable kind of pornographic website that it offers, and the ease with which adult videos can be obtained, have helped spread the mindset that all sex is good—in or out of marriage.

Barriers everywhere have dropped—and are still dropping as they near a complete collapse on all fronts. Seemingly, every day establishes new lows in immorality, perversion, debauchery and "anything goes" when it comes to sexual habits and appetites. Experimentation and indulgence have become the norm. Most today have come to believe that free sex of every conceivable kind, with the same or opposite sex—or both—is a simple matter of personal preference. It is as though there is no longer the slightest concern about whether sexual activity is *right* or *wrong*. Vast millions have come to believe that achieving sexual pleasure in any setting, for any purpose, and involving any kind of experimentation or activity (and this includes any number of men and women participating in a single sexual episode) is perfectly acceptable—and is now, at least unconsciously, even seen to be a kind of human "right" of sorts.

By every older human standard and definition of morality—not to mention what *God* teaches!—sexual values in the early twenty-first century are infinitely worse than a mere fifty years ago. Words like "disgusting," "sickening," "shocking" and "revolting" come to mind when one looks across the world at what is now seen to be almost normal conduct, at least in the eyes of young people. Even the bestiality more common in ancient times is quietly reappearing. It is not too early to ask: how soon before *this* perverse evil becomes at least tacitly accepted by society?

This Time Foretold

God foretold that in the "last days...men shall be...lovers of pleasures more than lovers of God" and "without natural affection" (II Tim. 3:1-4). In the age of gross materialism, mixed with rank hedonism, the three "L's" of *leisure*, *luxury* and *license* have come to dominate the thinking of whole societies and nations.

Of course, God is certainly not against enjoyment, which includes *many* kinds of pleasure, and obviously sex is perhaps chief among them. But He declares of our wanton, lascivious age, through the Old Testament prophet Jeremiah, that "Every one neighed after his neighbor's wife" (5:8). And it is in this context that the now almost completely forgotten Seventh Commandment prohibiting adultery is being routinely ignored by great numbers who then, as professing Christians, turn right around each week and go to church as though their conduct is of little or no consequence in God's sight. As one preacher so aptly put it: "Most people sow wild oats all week, and then go to church on Sunday and pray for a crop failure."

The Bible is filled with scriptures—literally scores of passages—describing the sexual saturation of wrong conduct and wrong thinking in the modern age. God pulls no punches in labeling many different kinds of sexual behavior as sin. A few of these will be examined more closely at the end of this chapter.

Rampant Adultery

Adultery is now rampant in all Western nations, with 83 percent of American households experiencing—and afflicted by—adultery, being committed by either one or both mates. The suffering of all kinds connected just to illicit sex by married people is staggering to consider. At what point will we find 90 percent—95 percent—or even 100 percent—of couples no longer faithful in marriage?

The widespread practice of adulterous "pleasure marriages" has grown stronger in the Middle East and is also quickly regaining popularity in the new, democratic Iraq. This is the custom of men marrying several so-called "widows" for the sole purpose of sex outside marriage, but done under the guise of taking care of women in need. In addition, because of China's explosion of economic prosperity, adultery in that country has grown so widespread that there are now tens of thousands of private investigators whose sole task is to track and report the marital infidelity of wealthy executives whose wives doubt their faithfulness. Incredibly, only one in 100 is found to be faithful! Then there are the various cultures of Europe, where having a mistress has long been considered a badge of honor—and wives willingly accept the status quo.

But conditions have gone far beyond simple adultery, which is wrong enough and terribly damaging. Recognize that the very worst kinds of perversion and sick, degenerate practices in modern society cannot even be discussed. The Bible actually prohibits such discussion: "For it is a shame even to speak of those things which are done of them in secret" (Eph. 5:12). It is important to bear in mind that the very worst things that are happening in the sexual arena throughout society are necessarily excluded here.

Many modern societies have been forced by militant social radicals to embrace the concept of political correctness. This mindset permits all people to live whatever lifestyle—including "alternative" ones—that they choose, as long as they can rationalize that "it doesn't hurt anyone else." Such tolerance was rarely, or possibly never, known before this age. Virtually everyone and everything that people do is now tolerated with little question. Of course, the arrival of the personal computer and the Internet has spawned and helped perpetuate this era of tolerance.

Pleasure and betterment for the self are the main goals and hopes of most people. In this vein, great numbers would argue that, if they are only hurting themselves, they should have the right to experiment and enjoy whatever they please. But is all this self-pleasure leading toward real betterment of lives? Absolutely not.

God Ordains Marriage

The most important human relationship—marriage—was first introduced in Genesis 2:18, when Eve was created: "And the Lord God said, It is not good that the man should be alone; I will make him an help meet for him."

Eve was created *after* Adam, not *with* him. God wanted to illustrate to Adam how incomplete and futile his life would be without a "help meet." Once Adam realized his need for human companionship, he could better appreciate having a wife. Eve's attributes were designed to complement Adam's. She was designed by God with the attributes needed to nurture and care for children. God made her suitable and fully compatible for Adam as his lifetime marriage partner.

Verse 24 states, "Therefore shall a man leave his father and his mother, and shall cleave unto his wife: and they shall be one flesh." Here, marriage is defined in greater detail. God created and ordained marriage as the union in which man and woman could be physically and emotionally fulfilled. Marriage was ordained to be a giving relationship with mutual love, care and consideration. God intended that man and woman mutually assist each other in the development of character. Marriage also serves as the basis for having and rearing children. Children were to be provided a safe haven and given many years of diligent training and supervision.

God intended that family life serve as the training ground for children. As children learn to obey and honor their parents, they will learn to obey and honor God. The father and mother's closeness and loyalty to each other helps children develop and succeed in an atmosphere of confidence and security.

In Colossians 3:18-19, Paul states, "Wives, submit yourselves unto your own husbands, as it is fit in the Lord. Husbands, love your wives, and be not bitter against them." Recognize that if these had not been common marital problems at that time, Paul would not have mentioned them in this letter. Whatever the cause for bitterness, generally the solution involves diligence in understanding and conciliation. This works if the husband loves his wife and she is submissive, as Christ commanded through Paul.

Christ and the Church

In Ephesians 5:22-23, Paul compares marriage to the relationship between Christ and the Church: "Wives, submit yourselves unto your own husbands, as unto the Lord. For the husband is the head of the wife, even as Christ is the Head of the Church: and He is the Savior of the body."

This is a profound statement! The husband must conduct himself toward his wife as Christ does toward His Church! A husband must nurture, guide, train and provide for his wife, just as Christ does for His Church!

Verses 24-25 and 28 further explain the analogy: "Therefore as the Church is subject unto Christ, so let the wives be to their own husbands in every thing. Husbands, love your wives, even as Christ also loved the Church, and gave Himself for it...So ought men to love their wives as their own bodies. He that loves his wife loves himself."

The two partners become one flesh (through marital relations) just as the Church is the body of Christ. "For we are members of His body, of His flesh, and of His bones. For this cause shall a man leave his father and mother, and shall be joined unto his wife, and they two shall be one flesh" (vs. 30-31).

Though the world is oblivious to this "great mystery," it is plainly written in verses 32-33: "This is a great mystery: but I speak concerning Christ and the church. Nevertheless let every one of you in particular so love his wife even as himself; and the wife see that she reverence her husband."

In recent times, this understanding was restored to the Church of God by a man named Herbert W. Armstrong, who stressed that the lesson of marriage was to ingrain faithfulness in God's Church. Thus, God's Church would be loyal to Christ for all eternity.

"You Are Not Your Own"

I Corinthians 6:15-17 reads, "Know you not that your bodies are the members of Christ? Shall I then take the members of Christ, and make them the members of an harlot [sexually immoral woman]? God forbid. What? Know you not that he which is joined to an harlot is one body? for two, says He, shall be one flesh. But he that is joined unto the Lord is one spirit." Becoming "one flesh" with a prostitute emphasizes the seriousness of adultery! Genesis 2:24 shows that husband and wife become "one flesh"—one marriage unit, as well as one in their sexual relationship. Adultery and fornication are serious for anyone—but especially those called by God to be part of Christ's spiritual body, His Church. Paul explains the foolishness of those actions, adding that Christians must exercise the power of God to rule over the pulls of the flesh.

I Corinthians 6:18-20 states, "Flee fornication. Every sin that a man does is without the body; but he that commits fornication sins against his own body. What? Know you not that your body is the temple of the Holy [Spirit] which is in you, which you have of God, and you are not your own? For you are bought with a price: therefore glorify God in your body, and in your spirit, which are God's."

How does a person sin against his own body? One aspect made evident in the above scriptures is that the husband's wife is actually his own flesh, and vice versa (Eph. 5:28-29; I Cor. 7:3-4). If he sins against his wife by committing adultery, he sins against himself. "Flee fornication" means to FLEE, just as Joseph did when confronted by Potiphar's wife in Genesis 39:7-12. We must not tolerate it and see how long we can resist this temptation. Those now called of God do not have claim over their own bodies. They have been bought and paid for by the sacrifice of Christ—*they are not their own!* A Christian must always remember this!

The Adultery-Idolatry Connection

Temptation and sexual seduction have long been integrated with idolatry in order to attract followers. Satan the devil has made adultery, fornication and sexual orgies part of the worship rituals in many pagan religions.

Numbers 25:1 records this history: "…the people began to commit whoredom with the daughters of Moab. And they called the people unto the sacrifice of their gods: and the people did eat, and bowed down to their gods. And Israel joined himself unto Baal-peor and the anger of the LORD was kindled against Israel."

In this account, many in Israel were being tempted by the deception of Balaam. He schemed a way to get God to curse Israel. Balaam arranged for thousands of beautiful Moabite and Midianite women to take part in a "religious" ceremony in the worship of Baal-peor. This sensual orgy was orchestrated to cause Israel to stumble and sin. Historical accounts point out that women involved in such pagan ceremonies were often forced to do this.

In ancient times, temple prostitutes were used to worship various pagan gods. The allure of the lust of the eyes and the lust of the flesh (I John 2:16) reinforced the attraction of idol worship. Notice the following quote (emphasis ours): "In Egypt, Phoenicia, Assyria, Chaldea, Canaan and Persia, the worship of Isis, Molech, Baal, Astarte, Mylitta, and other deities consisted of the most extravagant sensual orgies and the temples were merely centers of vice. In Babylon some degree of prostitution appears to have been even compulsory and imposed upon all women in honor of the goddess Mylitta. In India the ancient connection between religion and prostitution still survives… Among the Jews, who stood apart from the surrounding peoples, THE OBJECT OF THE MOSAIC LAW [the "laws of God," or the Ten Commandments] WAS CLEARLY TO PRESERVE THE PURITY OF THE RACE AND THE RELIGION" (*Encyclopedia Britannica*, 11th ed., Vol. 22, p. 458).

The following is from the same source and summarizes these historical observations: "Among the ancient nations of the East, WITH THE EXCEPTION OF THE JEWS, prostitution appears to have been connected with religious worship, and to have been not merely tolerated but encouraged." Only in the worship of the true God was this sexual perversion not found. When obeyed, God's laws protected Israel's purity.

Israel was more than willing to commit idolatry when adultery was included. Concerning this, Paul wrote in Colossians 3:5-6, "Mortify therefore your members which are upon the earth; fornication, uncleanness, inordinate affection, evil concupiscence, and covetousness, which is idolatry: for which things' sake the wrath of God comes on the children of disobedience."

Such lusts of the flesh are covetousness which, in turn, leads to idolatry—breaking the seventh, tenth and second commandments. Ephesians 5:5 confirms this: "For this you know, that no whoremonger, nor unclean person, nor covetous man, *who is an idolater*, has any inheritance in the kingdom of Christ and of God."

The wrath of God came upon those who committed adultery with the Moabite and Midianite women that Balaam had gathered. Numbers 25:9 shows that *24,000* died as a result of this sin.

The penalty of sin is death (Rom. 6:23). Leviticus 20:10 reads, "And the man that commits adultery with another man's wife, even he that commits adultery with his neighbor's wife, the adulterer and the adulteress shall surely be put to death." God promised swift and severe punishment for those who committed adultery. They became an example used to instill fear in others.

What Christ Taught

In Matthew 19, the Pharisees asked Jesus if it was lawful for a man to divorce his wife for any cause. He responded in verses 4-6, "Have you not read, that He which made them at the beginning made them male and female, and said, For this cause shall a man leave father and mother, and shall cleave to his wife: and they two shall be one flesh? Wherefore they are no more two, but one flesh. What therefore God has joined together, let not man put asunder."

Christ taught that the marriage vow was binding. The Pharisees quickly asked about the bill of divorcement that Moses allowed. Christ answered in verses 8-9, "Moses because of the hardness of your hearts suffered you to put away your wives: but from the beginning it was not so. And I say unto you, Whosoever shall put away his wife, except it be for fornication, and shall marry another, commits adultery: and whoso marries her which is put away does commit adultery."

As an apostle of Christ, Paul had the authority to clarify this. This clarification involved brethren in the Church who had been previously married to spouses who were unconverted and not in the Church. The unbelieving spouses had willingly departed, rejecting the beliefs of their converted mates. In these cases, the converted spouses were not bound (I Cor. 7:12-16). This clarification did not supersede Christ's words, but was an amendment for certain brethren who had come into God's Church.

Matthew 5:27-28 is a powerful statement with enormous implications: "You have heard that it was said by them of old time, You shall not commit adultery: But I say unto you, That whosoever looks on a woman to lust after her has committed adultery with her already in his heart."

Far from doing away with God's Law, Christ significantly expanded and magnified it. It is now far more binding—even one's thoughts are to be controlled, as opposed to obeying just the letter of the law. Though the world thinks that the Law is done away, God's people know it is still in effect.

So careful is the walk of a Christian that Paul had to caution the brethren in Ephesians 5:3-5, "But fornication, and all uncleanness, or covetousness, let it not be once named among you, as becomes saints; neither filthiness, nor foolish talking, nor jesting, which are not convenient: but rather giving of thanks. For this you know, that no whoremonger, nor unclean person, nor covetous man, who is an idolater, has any inheritance in the kingdom of Christ and of God."

From the Book of Proverbs

The Proverbs contain *many* additional admonitions and warnings about adultery, with some very extensive:

"Discretion shall preserve you, understanding shall keep you… To deliver you from the strange woman, even from the stranger which flatters with her words; which forsakes the guide of her youth, and forgets the covenant of her God. For her house inclines unto death, and her paths unto the dead. None that go unto her return again, neither take they hold of the paths of life" (2:11, 16-19).

"For the lips of a strange woman drop as an honeycomb, and her mouth is smoother than oil: But her end is bitter as wormwood, sharp as a two-edged sword. Her feet go down to death; her steps take hold on hell. Lest you should ponder the path of life, her ways are moveable, that you cannot know them. Hear me now therefore, O you children, and depart not from the words of my mouth. Remove your way far from her, and come not near the door of her house: lest you give your honor unto others, and your years unto the cruel: lest strangers be filled with your wealth; and your labors be in the house of a stranger; and you mourn at the last, when your flesh and your body are consumed, and say, How have I hated instruction, and my heart despised reproof; and have not obeyed the voice of my teachers, nor inclined mine ear to them that instructed me! I was almost in all evil in the midst of the congregation and assembly" (5:3-14).

"And why will you, my son, be ravished with a strange woman, and embrace the bosom of a stranger?" (5:20).

"For the commandment is a lamp; and the law is light; and reproofs of instruction are the way of life: to keep you from the evil woman, from the flattery of the tongue of a strange woman. Lust not after her beauty in your heart; neither let her take you with her eyelids. For by means of a whorish woman a man is brought to a piece of bread: and the adulteress will hunt for the precious life. Can a man take fire in his bosom, and his clothes not be burned? Can one go upon hot coals, and his feet not be burned? So he that goes in to his neighbor's wife; whosoever touches her shall not be innocent. Men do not despise a thief, if he steal to satisfy his soul when he is hungry; but if he be found, he shall restore sevenfold; he shall give all the substance of his house. But whoso commits adultery with a woman lacks understanding: he that doeth it destroys his own soul. A wound and dishonor shall he get; and his reproach shall not be wiped away. For jealousy is the rage of a man: therefore he will not spare in the day of vengeance. He will not regard any ransom; neither will he rest content, though you give many gifts" (6:23-35).

Also take the time to read Proverbs 7:4-27; 9:13-18; 5:15-19; 18:22; 19:14.

Solomon's Experience

King Solomon, who possessed great wealth and was in a position to fulfill every conceivable desire of his heart, made some profound observations (Ecc. 1:13). He learned many lessons by way of experience. We can benefit from his wisdom.

Solomon had 700 wives and 300 concubines—1,000 of the most beautiful women in the world. He observed that trying to satisfy carnal lusts was an exercise in futility. He saw that lust was equal to grasping an illusion. God allowed Solomon to go to these lengths and to record them for our benefit. It is better to learn from his example than to make the same mistakes.

Solomon finally concluded, "All things are full of labor; man cannot utter it: the eye is not satisfied with seeing, nor the ear filled with hearing" (Ecc. 1:8). Ecclesiastes 5:10 continues, "He that loves silver shall not be satisfied with silver; nor he that loves abundance with increase: this is also vanity."

We can take his word for it, since he spoke from experience, not from wistful hopes or wishes. Whatever one lusts after, he would never be satisfied with it—be it 1,000 of the world's most beautiful women or fabulous wealth. Though Solomon had all this and had accomplished great things, he lamented, "Therefore I hated life; because the work that is wrought under the sun is grievous unto me: for all is vanity and vexation of spirit" (Ecc. 2:17).

Here was his conclusion, repeated from the book's introduction: "Let us hear the *conclusion* of the whole matter: Fear God, and keep His commandments: for this is the whole duty of man" (Ecc. 12:13). The phrase "duty of" was inserted by translators, the reason for its being found in italics. The last phrase should simply be, "for this is the whole man." Fearing God and keeping His commandments are to be ingrained into the innermost being.

This key principle is also found in Leviticus 18:5: "You shall therefore keep My statutes, and My judgments: which if a man do, he shall live in them: I am the LORD."

Solomon paid dearly for these experiences, as recorded in I Kings 11:4: "For it came to pass, when Solomon was old, that his wives turned away his heart after other gods: and his heart was not perfect with the LORD his God, as was the heart of David his father." Verse 11 continues, "Wherefore the LORD said unto Solomon, Forasmuch as this is done of you, and you have not kept My covenant and My statutes, which I have commanded you, I will surely rend the kingdom from you, and will give it to your servant."

Solomon's actions brought *consequences*. The same is true for anyone today!

Moral Collapse

God warns against moral permissiveness: "Do not prostitute your daughter, to cause her to be a whore; lest the land fall to whoredom, and the land become full of wickedness" (Lev. 19:29). God shows that prostitution results in the land becoming full of wickedness. Every other form of evil follows its wake. Modern society bears stark testimony to this.

Occasionally, news broadcasts will show a group of residents protesting against a strip club or a massage parlor moving into their neighborhood. It is generally known that these elements bring with them other vices, such as more open prostitution, drug rings, organized crime, homicides, theft and other crimes of opportunity. General corruption fills their neighborhood.

Wickedness breeds more wickedness, which leads to moral collapse. Here is what God instructed: "Moreover you shall not lie carnally with your neighbor's wife, to defile yourself with her. And you shall not let any of your seed pass through the fire to Molech, neither shall you profane the name of your God: I am the Lord. You shall not lie with mankind, as with womankind: it is abomination. Neither shall you lie with any beast to defile yourself therewith…it is confusion. Defile not you yourselves in *any* of these things: for in all these the nations are defiled which I cast out before you" (Lev. 18:20-24).

These verses make it clear that God not only condemns homosexuality, but He also calls it an *abomination*. Bestiality is also forbidden and is simply called "confusion."

God then admonished Israel to avoid this wickedness and its consequences: "And the land is defiled: therefore I do visit the iniquity thereof upon it, and the land itself vomits out her inhabitants. You shall therefore keep My statutes and My judgments, and shall not commit any of these abominations; neither any of your own nation, nor any stranger that sojourns among you: (For all these abominations have the men of the land done, which were before you, and the land is defiled;) That the land spew not you out also, when you defile it, as it spewed out the nations that were before you" (vs. 25-28).

Today's liberal educators, politicians, entertainers, media stars, and clergy promote "political correctness," including acceptance of homosexuality. Anyone who disagrees with them is usually labeled a "homophobe" and a bigot. Just as nature itself teaches that it is a shame for a man to have long hair, so also does it cry out against *these* abominations. Those who are deeply warped into such behavioral patterns are often not salvageable in this life.

People, like nations, can morally collapse and corrupt others. God can and will eventually redeem the vast majority of these people and they will learn to honor His ways. Tragically, today's liberal concept of mercy is co-existence with sin and perversion. But God has a much better plan in store for the recovery of those who have self-destructed in this life.

Great Purpose Revealed!

The world has been ignorant of the true purposes of sex. The result has been untold pain and suffering for the masses! This misery—now epidemic—is measured in disease, new kinds of perversion, unwanted pregnancies yielding abortions, illegitimate children or unwanted children in marriage, sky-rocketing divorce rates, which in turn produce corresponding numbers of jumbled families, bankruptcies, court battles and even crime.

Sadly, these conditions grow worse and more complicated, with each new generation compounding the problems and evils of the previous one.

Tragedy, unhappiness and confusion about sex and marriage have afflicted every nation of the world for thousands of years, and people have not known where to turn for the answers—the solutions—to so many ill effects, now running rampant.

The Seventh Commandment is written for those who will consider what Almighty God instructs, not for the willingly disobedient. God reveals that marriage and sex have a marvelous purpose completely beyond the bounds of human imagination. After hearing God's explanation, you be the judge of whether it makes more sense than that which is offered by evolutionists and traditional Christianity.

There is another aspect of the Seventh Commandment that must at least be referenced before this brief chapter is complete. Remember, in regard to adultery, if you will not accept God's revealed Word, you are left with no choice but to be ignorant of how and when marriage began, and of the purposes of sex. You must accept that marriage is either a human invention on the road of evolution, or the falsehood of religion—that it is for no purpose other than procreation because celibacy is a "higher calling." These are your only options!

With either, the marvelous answers available in God's Word to the great questions of marriage and sex remain shrouded in mystery.

We have available a number of books and booklets on the subject of marriage, sex, dating and courtship and related topics. To understand a great deal more, consider reading the following books: *Sex – Its Unknown Dimension* and *Dating and Courtship – God's Way*. There are also three booklets that are most informative: *The Purpose of Marriage – Ever Obsolete?*, *You Can Build a Happy Marriage* and *Understanding Divorce and Remarriage*.

What If...?

The same question repeats itself: what if the whole world kept the Seventh Commandment? Adultery would not exist. People would consider the long-term consequences of their actions.

Almost every television program and movie would have to rewrite their scripts. Advertising would have to find a new theme to sell everything from ratchet wrench sets to used tires without their traditional sex pitch. Magazines would have to do the same. The Internet's biggest moneymaker and fastest growing business—(ever-worsening) pornography—would collapse!

Further, there would be no more prostitution, strip clubs, adult movie theaters, exotic sex shops, or escort services. Extramarital affairs would not exist, drastically affecting the divorce rate, sending many children into a much happier future. Illegitimate births and sexually transmitted diseases would disappear. Sexually suggestive clothing styles, which lead to a variety of sexual sins and crimes, would all disappear. And the list goes on.

All these changes and more will be effectively implemented in the coming millennial utopia, when Satan's influences are gone.

The Eighth Commandment— "You Shall Not Steal"

Next, God thundered the Eighth Commandment, recorded in Exodus 20:15: "YOU SHALL NOT STEAL."

To obey this command is to respect the property and possessions of others. It also entails the way people are to conduct business. God's Way is honesty, fairness, and justice in all dealings, including every facet of finances and accounting.

Stealing Brings Consequences

God views stealing as an act of deception, which is lying. In Leviticus 19:11, 13, stealing is classified: "You shall not steal, neither deal falsely, neither lie one to another...You shall not defraud your neighbor, neither rob him: the wages of him that is hired shall not abide with you all night until the morning." God's laws protect those who, through hard work, seek to make an honest living. The violators of His law were to be punished with swift justice, thus instilling fear in many potential thieves and scam artists.

As part of the punishment, God required that the thief pay *more* than the original value of what was taken. The amount was to be determined by judges, but in some cases, was set in law. Exodus 22:1 explains how this was usually applied: "If a man shall steal an ox, or a sheep, and kill it, or sell it; he shall restore five oxen for an ox, and four sheep for a sheep."

The thief was at greater risk in Israel because he forfeited any protection of his life under the law. "If a thief be found breaking up, and be smitten that he die, there shall no blood be shed for him" (vs. 2). God's laws protected and benefited the victim. On the other hand, modern laws tend to favor the perpetrators, who are often the ones portrayed as the victims. Today, we are far removed from God's way of justice. People of the liberal establishment, well entrenched in the judiciary systems of this world, make themselves out to be more righteous than God.

In ancient Israel, the penalty for kidnapping was death. Notice: "If a man be found stealing any of his brethren of the children of Israel, and makes merchandise of him, or sells him [slavery]; then that thief shall die; and you shall put evil away from among you" (Deut. 24:7). God allowed no loopholes for liberal judges or lawyers, who thrive in our day. The penalty for kidnapping or any other transgression was fixed and non-negotiable. Everyone knew exactly what was at stake when they considered committing a crime. Although capital punishment is viewed as harsh by many today, this is meant to act as a deterrent against crime. God reveals that this is how a nation removes evil from being a problem.

Certain classes of people are generally vulnerable to theft and deception. The elderly are usually preyed upon by scam artists. The poor are usually sought out by petty thieves. In Isaiah 10:1-2, God chastised Israel for not defending the poor and needy whom God put in their care: "Woe unto them that decree unrighteous decrees, and that write grievousness which they have prescribed; to turn aside the needy from judgment, and to take away the right from the poor of My people, that widows may be their prey, and that they may rob the fatherless!"

When God condemned ancient Israel or Judah for wickedness, stealing was usually listed first among their sins. Take Jeremiah 7:8-10, for example: "Behold, you trust in lying words, that cannot profit. Will you steal, murder, and commit adultery, and swear falsely, and burn incense unto Baal, and walk after other gods whom you know not; and come and stand before Me in this house, which is called by My name, and say, We are delivered to do all these abominations?"

It is remarkable how this rebuke against Judah, shortly before the Babylonian captivity, fits the mentality of self-professing Christians today. Most of those who attend the major denominations consider themselves "delivered" to do as they please—to break the laws of God with impunity. They believe that righteousness is imputed to them, through grace, regardless of their *conduct*. Paul directly states that grace is not a license to sin and claim immunity (Rom. 6:1-2). (We will look at this in much more detail in Chapter Fifteen.)

Withholding the wages of a hired worker is also stealing. Many employers practice this deceit. James 5:4-6 states, "Behold, the hire of the laborers who have reaped down your fields, which is of you kept back by fraud, cries: and the cries of them which have reaped are entered into the ears of the Lord of Sabaoth [Sabbath]. You have lived in pleasure on the earth, and been wanton; you have nourished your hearts, as in a day of slaughter. You have condemned and killed the just; and he does not resist you."

This powerful rebuke is a slap in the face to any who conclude that, as long as one just has "love," there is no obligation to their fellow man.

New Testament Teachings

Here is Paul's clear admonition to the Church: "Let him that stole steal no more: but rather let him labor, working with his hands the thing which is good, that he may have to give to him that needs" (Eph. 4:28). Paul understood that before learning the truth and coming into the Church, many had violated the Eighth Commandment. He admonished them never to steal again, but to provide for themselves and others through honest hard work. Paul stressed the necessity of honest hard labor in providing for one's dependents.

A thief's motives and actions are completely opposed to the way of Christ. Notice: "The thief comes not, but for to steal, and to kill, and to destroy: I am come that they might have life, and that they might have it more abundantly" (John 10:10). Realize that a thief comes to *get* for himself and to take as he sees fit. Christ, on the other hand, came to *give*. And He gave the principles by which His followers can have abundant life.

Romans 2:21 makes a serious charge: "You therefore which teaches another, teach you not yourself? You that preach a man should not steal, do you steal?" Paul was addressing the Jews as teachers, since they had been schooled in the law. Yet the message applies to any who have the opportunity to teach. They are held accountable by Christ to "practice what they preach."

Tithes and Offerings Belong to God

God commands that we pay tithes and give offerings. To withhold either of these is stealing from God. Carefully read Malachi 3:8-12: "Will a man rob God? Yet you have robbed Me. But you say, Wherein have we robbed You? In tithes and offerings. You are cursed with a curse: for you have robbed Me, even this whole nation. Bring you all the tithes into the storehouse, that there may be meat in Mine house, and prove Me now herewith, says the LORD of hosts, if I will not open you the windows of heaven, and pour you out a blessing, that there shall not be room enough to receive it. And I will rebuke the devourer [this means crop-destroying insects] for your sakes, and he shall not destroy the fruits of your ground; neither shall your vine cast her fruit before the time in the field, says the LORD of hosts. And all nations shall call you blessed: for you shall be a delightsome land, says the LORD of hosts."

The penalty for withholding the tithes that belong to God is an automatic curse upon the whole nation. (Read our thorough booklet *End All Your Financial Worries*.)

God inspired Malachi to write of the blessings that occur upon paying God's tithes. In the statement, "and all nations shall call you blessed," God is saying, in effect, "Stop stealing from Me and see if I will not bless you with great abundance." This is an offer that no individual or nation should pass up.

From the Book of Proverbs

The proverbs below pertain to honesty and integrity, and deceit, theft, robbery and casting lots:

"He that by usury and unjust gain increases his substance, he shall gather it for him that will pity the poor" (28:8).

"A wicked man takes a gift out of the bosom to pervert the ways of judgment" (17:23).

"Rob not the poor, because he is poor: neither oppress the afflicted in the gate" (22:22).

"Whoso is partner with a thief hates his own soul: he hears cursing, and betrays it not" (29:24).

"The lot is cast into the lap; but the whole disposing thereof is of the LORD" (16:33).

Also read Proverbs 6:30; 11:1; 16:11; 18:18; 20:10, 23; 21:7; 22:28; 23:10-11; 29:4.

An Unrecognized Form of Robbery

The following is an insightful and fascinating statement from Herbert W. Armstrong's article "Does God Exist?," which was printed in *The Plain Truth* Magazine, in June 1972:

"But now let's COMPARE the wisdom and intelligence of man with that of GOD who brought these marvels into being, and keeps them functioning.

"The grain of wheat GOD causes to grow out of the ground is a perfect food. But, like other perfect gifts from God, man fails to value the priceless perfection of the all-wise God, and, undertaking to improve on God's handiwork, perverts, pollutes, and defiles it! Every bit of God's perfection man's hand has ever touched, it would seem, he has besmirched, spoiled and polluted!

"And the poor, defenseless grain of wheat is no exception! Into flour mills of human devising go the millions of bushels of healthful wheat. And there the supposedly intelligent human takes it apart, removes the alkaline-reacting mineral elements, and turns out for human consumption sacks of white flour composed largely of the acid-reacting carbohydrate elements—with poison bleach added!

"Out of this, the human population makes healthless bread, biscuits, doughnuts, pastries, puddings, macaroni, spaghetti, gravies, etc., etc., often mixing flour with 'refined' sugar and greases or fats—a combination guaranteed to wreck any organism in time! Yes, the sugar refiners do the same thing to sugar; and nearly all foods on the market for human consumption today have gone through man's factories and suffered from man's processes until they have been devitalized, depleted of their health-giving nutrients, and turned from foods into slow-acting poisons! And these foodless foods with which man has tampered in lust for profits have produced in human bodies a whole series of diseases of which our forefathers of a few generations ago had never heard! There is a reason why the history of degenerative diseases has paralleled the rise of modern technology!

"Today human beings drop dead before their time with heart failure; others die with cancer; the population suffers rheumatism, arthritis, diabetes, kidney diseases, anemia, colds, fevers, pneumonia, and thousands of other diseases. We respond to the toothbrush and toothpaste ads and frantically brush our teeth, but our teeth keep decaying, and we lose them beginning at an early age because of a lack of calcium and other elements in our diet.

"It would seem man is not very intelligent after all!

"Then, too, the God who created this earth and all vegetation told us to let our land lie idle every seventh year. But man is too greedy to do that. And so our land is worn out and depleted, and natural good foods such as carrots, beets, and turnips are lacking in the necessary mineral elements and vitamins! And drug companies get rich selling vitamin pills!

"Whose intelligence is higher—that of the GOD who provided every perfect need for every living thing or that of greedy, gullible, God-rejecting humans who in the interest of bigger profits and more luxuries for themselves have ROBBED the very foods which God created and gave us, of their health- and body-building values?"

What If...?

Yet again, we consider the big picture: If the entire world kept the Eighth Commandment, many dramatic changes would result. Most locks would no longer be needed. The remaining locks would be used to signal privacy or to detain prisoners convicted of *other* crimes. Armored cars would be obsolete. So would security guards. Theft-related homicides would no longer exist. There would be no need for burglar alarms or steering wheel locks.

Prices in department and discount stores would drop significantly due to the removal of the built-in cushions to cover the cost of shoplifting (called "shrinkage"). Home, car, and business insurance would also drop significantly. Businesses would be more equitable to workers and they would be diligent to honestly work for their pay. Labor unions would not be needed, since workers and employers would be cooperating in a spirit of equity. The elderly would no longer have to be on guard against scam artists that specialize in wiping out their life savings. Bribery, extortion and "white collar" crimes would no longer exist. The world would be a much better place without stealing and robbery.

In such a world, instead of the *way of get*, the benefit-rich *way of give* would predominate.

The Ninth Commandment—
"You Shall Not
Bear False Witness..."

God gives the NINTH COMMANDMENT in Exodus 20:16: "YOU SHALL NOT BEAR FALSE WITNESS AGAINST YOUR NEIGHBOR."

This commandment condemns all manner of lying and deception—*every* form. This includes outright lying, false advertising, slander, shading the truth, even exaggerating, as well as false testimony in a court of law. Justice can only be based on truth. (Of course, truth extends far beyond judicial proceedings.)

Truth embodies the very character of God—all that He is and does. God's character is so perfect—but also so powerful—that He literally *cannot* lie (Heb. 6:18). He wants all mankind to learn the value of truth in every aspect of life.

Judgment for False Witnesses

Exodus 23:1-2 reads, "You shall not raise a false report: put not your hand with the wicked to be an unrighteous witness. You shall not follow a multitude to do evil [i.e., *riots*]; neither shall you speak in a cause to decline after many to wrest judgment [i.e., *collusion* or *scheming*]."

Notice Deuteronomy 19:15, which diminished the chance of false accusations: "One witness shall not rise up against a man for any iniquity, or for any sin, in any sin that he sins: at the mouth of two witnesses, or at the mouth of three witnesses, shall the matter be established." Two or three witnesses were always required to establish a charge before a judge.

Next, the judges had to *diligently* examine the individual bringing the charges. Notice: "If a false witness rise up against any man to testify against him that which is wrong; then both the men, between whom the controversy is, shall stand before the LORD, before the priests and the judges, which shall be in those days; and the judges shall make diligent inquisition: and, behold, if the witness be a false witness, and has testified falsely against his brother; then shall you do unto him, as he had thought to have done unto his brother: so shall you put the evil away from among you. and those which remain shall hear, and fear, and shall henceforth commit no more any such evil among you" (vs. 16-20).

God's judgments far exceed those of man. God looks at the long-term effects, while man only looks at the short term.

The Trend in Israel and Judah

When any or all of the tribes of Israel rebelled and rejected the words of God's prophets, lying and falsehood reigned. Notice Isaiah 30:9: "That this is a rebellious people, lying children, children that will not hear the law of the LORD." Liars would naturally avoid hearing this law because they are condemned by it.

Notice this strong indictment from Isaiah 59:4, 13: "None calls for justice, nor any pleads for truth: they trust in vanity, and speak lies; they conceive mischief, and bring forth iniquity...In transgressing and lying against the LORD, and departing away from our God, speaking oppression and revolt, conceiving and uttering from the heart words of falsehood."

Israel's historic tendency to seek out and listen to false prophets is also condemned in Jeremiah 7:8: "Behold, you trust in lying words, that cannot profit." In fact, almost everyone today is forced to trust (meaning, to believe) liars.

Now compare David's attitude as he wrote the following Psalms. Some of them reveal man's deceitfulness, while others exalt the truthfulness of God's Way:

"I have hated them that regard lying vanities: but I trust in the LORD" (31:6).

"Let the lying lips be put to silence; which speak grievous things proudly and contemptuously against the righteous" (31:18).

"For the sin of their mouth and the words of their lips let them even be taken in their pride: and for cursing and lying which they speak" (59:12).

"For the mouth of the wicked and the mouth of the deceitful are opened against me: they have spoken against me with a lying tongue" (109:2).

"Remove from me the way of lying: and grant me Your law graciously" (119:29).

"I hate and abhor lying: but Your law do I love" (119:163).

"Deliver my soul, O LORD, from lying lips, and from a deceitful tongue" (120:2).

The Truth in Perspective

Christians must follow God's Spirit. "Howbeit when He [It], the *Spirit of truth*, is come, He [It] will guide you into all truth" (John 16:13). In prayer to God, Christ stated, "Sanctify them [those whom God committed unto Christ] through your *truth*, YOUR WORD IS TRUTH" (John 17:17). In John 14:5, Thomas asked, "How can we know the way?" Jesus replied, "I am the way, *the truth*, and the life" (vs. 6). God the Father and Christ personify truth.

In contrast to God, whose way is embodied in truth, notice the way of the devil. In John 8:44, Christ condemned the Pharisees, who refused to accept His word. Notice: "You are of your father the devil, and the lusts of your father you will do. He was a murderer from the beginning, and abode not in the truth, because there is *no truth* in him. When he speaks a lie, he speaks of his own: *for he is a liar, and the father of it.*"

This scripture explains why false religion, engineered and orchestrated by Satan, is deeply embodied in deceit. Every entity that opposes God's Way operates on the principles of treachery, deceit and falsehood—the antithesis of truth.

Verses 31-32 reveal a profound concept about truth: "Then said Jesus to those Jews which believed on Him, If you continue in My word, then are you My disciples indeed; and you shall know the truth, and the truth shall make you free." The Jews felt that they were already free. Christ explained that they were actually servants of sin—so is anyone who sins as a way of life.

One of the greatest assets that a Christian can have is the desire to *seek the truth*. As one *speaks the truth* and exerts effort to *live by*

the truth, he will come to *acknowledge the truth* when he is correct-
ed. When a person does this, in spite of weaknesses and imperfec-
tions, God can easily work with him, like clay in the hands of a pot-
ter. To grow and develop, one must become, and remain, *anchored to
the truth*.

Paul taught that we must control the tendency to lie and exagger-
ate the truth. Consider his words: "Wherefore putting away lying,
speak every man truth with his neighbor: for we are members one of
another" (Eph. 4:25). Also, "Lie not one to another, seeing that you
have put off the old man with his deeds" (Col. 3:9). In order to overcome the carnal inclination to lie, one must realize its futility and the
danger of its consequences.

However, God's Spirit and obeying God's laws will help you to
overcome this.

Revelation 21:8 reveals the ultimate fate of all who will not repent of lying: "But the fearful, and unbelieving, and the abominable,
and murderers, and whoremongers, and sorcerers, and idolaters, *and
all liars*, shall have their part in the lake which burns with fire and
brimstone: which is the second death."

From the Book of Proverbs

This list contains proverbs that address truthfulness and deceit:

"These six things does the LORD hate: yes, seven are an abomination unto Him: a proud look, a lying tongue, and hands that shed innocent blood, an heart that devises wicked imaginations, feet that be
swift in running to mischief, a false witness that speaks lies, and he
that sows discord among brethren" (6:16-19).

"He that hides hatred with lying lips, and he that utters a slander,
is a fool" (10:18).

"He that speaks truth shows forth righteousness: but a false witness deceit. There is that speaks like the piercing of a sword: but the
tongue of the wise is health. The lip of truth shall be established for
ever: but a lying tongue is but for a moment. Deceit is in the heart of
them that imagine evil: but to the counselors of peace is joy" (12:17-
20).

"Lying lips are abomination to the LORD: but they that deal truly
are His delight" (12:22).

"A righteous man hates lying: but a wicked man is loathsome,
and cometh to shame" (13:5).

"A faithful witness will not lie: but a false witness will utter lies" (14:5).

Also read these Proverbs: 17:7; 19:5, 9; 21:6; 25:18; 26:28.

What If...?

We revisit the same great question: what if the entire world obeyed the Ninth Commandment? There would be no more lying. There would be no more propaganda from politicians and world leaders. Everyone could believe *every* word of the news, as well as from advertisements. Exaggerations, distortions and half-truths would give way to the full truth. Every conversation and every business dealing would be honest—void of all forms of deceit.

All slander and character assassination would cease. People would be known for what they truly are, instead of what is perceived about them because of slander or gossip. People would no longer put up false fronts. Con men and scam artists would disappear.

All this is prophesied to occur in Christ's 1,000-year rule, as revealed in Isaiah 32:5-6: "The vile person shall be no more called liberal [generous], nor the churl [crude, selfish] said to be bountiful. For the vile person will speak villany, and his heart will work iniquity [lawlessness], to practice hypocrisy."

The Tenth Commandment—
"You Shall Not Covet..."

God's voice thundered the TENTH COMMANDMENT in Exodus 20:17: "YOU SHALL NOT COVET your neighbor's house, you shall not covet your neighbor's wife, nor his manservant, nor his maidservant, nor his ox, nor his ass, *nor anything that is your neighbor's.*"

The word "covet" comes from the Hebrew word *chamad*, which means "to desire or lust for something pleasant or of precious value." It is easy to understand why God does not want anyone to desire someone else's wife or house. But what about the other things listed in this command?

Although a manservant was a bondman, or servant, of the owner, he was often more than a common laborer. He may have been a skilled supervisor of other servants and of sizeable herds or flocks owned by his master. Likewise, the maidservant may have been an irreplaceable manager of many functions of a home, like tutoring, or weaving fabric for clothing. The value of these servants was great. They could make the difference in a successful household.

The value of an ox was also significant. Large and powerful, oxen were usually put in teams to pull wagons or plows. Even the beef from such a large animal was valuable. The ass was another valuable animal and a tireless worker. They were larger than donkeys but slightly smaller than horses. Asses were more commonly used in Israel than other animals, such as mules, which were products of hybrid breeding and forbidden in Israel (Lev. 19:19).

The last thing mentioned is "anything that is your neighbor's." This covers everything else belonging to your neighbor.

The total of the items listed is seven. In the Bible, the number seven signifies *perfection* and *completion*. Perhaps this is why God listed this many items. God allows no loopholes for man to covet anything that someone else possesses. Of course, it is not wrong for someone to desire a mate. But to desire *someone else's* mate is prohibited. The world has yet to learn this lesson.

Covetousness in Perspective

Paul upheld the Law of God and explained this in Romans 7:7, "What shall we say then? Is the law sin? God forbid. No, I had not known sin, but by the law: for I had not known lust, except the law had said, *You shall not covet*." Now consider verse 14: "For we know that the law is spiritual: but I am carnal, sold under sin." Most do not think of the Ten Commandments as spiritual in nature, but rather as "do's and don'ts" pertaining to the letter of the law. But they are much more than this.

Remember that Christ magnified the commandment against killing to show that anyone who even harbors *hatred* for another is as guilty as a murderer. He also showed that anyone who even *lusts* after a woman is guilty of adultery. Christ expanded the letter of the law to include the control of thoughts—the innermost being, or the heart. The Tenth Commandment is unique. It deals with the innermost thoughts of people and *spiritual* thinking toward *physical* things. For example, you could obey the Eighth Commandment by merely not stealing. However, the Tenth Commandment forbids people from even *thinking about* stealing—and, of course, just desiring things that belong to someone else.

Satan, as the god of this world (II Cor. 4:4), and the "prince of the power of the air" (Eph. 2:2), broadcasts *his* attitudes, such as coveting. Human beings are naturally "tuned in" to the attitudes of the devil's wavelength. Only with God's Holy Spirit can you develop the self-control to "tune them out." (You may wish to read our booklet *Did God Create Human Nature?*)

Those who succumb to addiction have, in effect, failed to control their lust for sex, alcohol, drugs, adultery, gambling, video games or anything else—and there are a host of others almost too numerous to count. This could also apply to television, videos, the Internet or music. With the power of God's Spirit, determination and persistence, these can be overcome.

Here is how Paul cautioned those who were in the process of overcoming: "But fornication, and all uncleanness, or covetousness, let it not be once named among you, as becomes saints; neither filthiness, nor foolish talking, nor jesting, which are not convenient: but rather giving of thanks. For this you know, that no whoremonger, nor unclean person, nor covetous man, who is an idolater, has any inheritance in the kingdom of Christ and of God" (Eph. 5:3-5).

In avoiding temptation, Proverbs 6:25 warns, "Lust not after her beauty in your heart; neither let her take you with her eyelids."

All actions spring from thoughts. In fact, we *are* what we *think*. This is why David meditated upon God's perfect law. He sought to think like God thinks. Carefully read Psalms 119 in its entirety, perhaps on your knees and ask God to help you appreciate what He appreciates, just as David did. On this theme, Philippians 2:5 states, "Let this mind be in you, which was also in Christ Jesus."

Overcoming means literally "bringing into captivity every thought to the obedience of Christ" (II Cor. 10:5). (Chapter Seventeen will cover this process of overcoming—and preventing sin in the first place—in a much more thorough way.)

Biblical Examples

God required that all leaders who were selected to assist Moses meet certain qualifications: "Moreover you shall provide out of all the people able men, such as fear God, men of truth, *hating covetousness*; and place such over them, to be rulers of thousands, and rulers of hundreds, rulers of fifties, and rulers of tens" (Ex. 18:21).

Proverbs 28:16 states, "The prince that wants understanding is also a great oppressor: *but he that hates covetousness shall prolong his days.*"

In giving guidelines to Timothy about qualifications for bishops (ministers) and deacons, Paul stressed that they must be "*not greedy of filthy lucre*" (I Tim 3:3, 8). Greed for money is probably the most common type of lust and would undermine one's ability to assume greater responsibility.

To people consumed with greed for money and all it represents, Jesus admonished, "*Take heed, and beware of covetousness: for a man's life consists not in the abundance of the things which he pos-*

sesses" (Luke 12:15). He also inspired Paul to write, "Let your conversation [conduct] be *without covetousness*; and be content with such things as you have" (Heb. 13:5). Of course, this is important instruction for every human being. Always strive to be content with what you have and you will prevent covetousness.

David prayed, "Incline my heart unto Your testimonies, and not to *covetousness*" (Psa. 119:36). Learn to express this often in prayer, and remember it the next time you are facing temptation.

God condemned Judah for turning away from Him in Jeremiah 6:13: "For from the least of them even unto the greatest of them every one is given to *covetousness*; and from the prophet even unto the priest every one deals falsely." This is repeated in Jeremiah 8:10.

The prophet Ezekiel writes this about those who live at the end of the age just prior to Christ's Return: "And they come unto you as the people comes, and they sit before you as My people, and they hear your words, but they will not do them: for with their mouth they show much love, but *their heart goes after their covetousness*" (33:31).

Sadly, the covetousness of this materialistic world prevents most who hear God's truth from acting upon it.

Notice what Paul stated in Galatians 5:16: "This I say then, Walk in the Spirit, and you shall not fulfill the lust of the flesh." Then the apostle Peter adds this: "Whereby are given unto us exceeding great and precious promises: that by these you might be partakers of the divine nature, having escaped the corruption that is in the world through lust" (II Peter 1:4).

And John wrote, "For all that is in the world, the *lust* of the flesh, and the *lust* of the eyes, and the pride of life, is not of the Father, but is of the world. And the world passes away, and the *lust* thereof: but he that does the will of God abides for ever" (I John 2:16-17).

These scriptures explain our natural vulnerability to *lust*. The way to overcome this is through God working within the mind.

Other Forms of Coveting

Although the Bible contains no *direct* laws concerning gambling, those who earnestly seek to follow God will see that the principle opposes God's ways, just as much as stealing. When a person gambles, his entire approach is based on the way of *get*, which is contrary to God's way of GIVE.

Gambling casinos appeal to the lusts of people who desire to "hit it big" and "get something for nothing." They lust for riches, relying on *luck* rather than on *God*. Nowhere does God wish us "the best of luck." If we obey His laws, we can expect Him to bless us. But disobedience brings curses. Luck is not even in the picture.

Lacking self-control, a great many people have become addicted to gambling, in many cases losing all their assets. Any activity that gives way to lust should be avoided. This includes all forms of gambling—horse and dog races, card games with stakes, lotteries, sweepstakes, any "get rich scheme" in which there is a risk of personal loss, and even office pools.

A close look at the various cities around the world where gambling casinos thrive reveals a host of problems. Invariably, prostitution, organized crime, homicides and drugs are rampant. These things are all based on lust and greed.

Some ask God to bless them in winning a lottery or sweepstakes, since they barely make ends meet and need help to get out of debt. So many fail to realize that God does not—and would never—bless anything that is contrary to His Law!

Throughout the Bible, examples can be found of God's servants casting lots as a solemn appeal to Him to decide a doubtful matter according to *His* will. But God's people should never cast lots for the purpose of *gambling*. This terribly cheapens and perverts God's right use of lots.

It is God's will that people learn to trust and look to Him, while following His ways and laws. This is how character is developed. If God were to "bless" His people with "jackpot winnings," they would quickly amass too many material possessions, while probably losing the focus of developing His holy, righteous character—the Christian's very purpose for being.

Many proverbs discuss the importance of employing diligence in all the affairs of this life. Certainly, a Christian is not expected to be a pauper (Matt. 6:33). But it is only through hard work and perseverance that the diligent person will grow his fortune.

What If...?

We ask the same question of the final commandment: what if the entire world kept the Tenth Commandment? With no more lust and covetousness, idolatry and adultery would greatly diminish. But this would be just the beginning. Lust-driven consumerism would disappear, and along with it, consumer debt and bankruptcy.

More people would drive affordable vehicles, instead of going into debt to buy something that appeals to lustful vanity and pride. In short, materialism and impulse buying would vanish, as would all credit card debt, which results.

The entire world will soon learn that only with the help of God's Spirit can mankind successfully control lust and keep the Tenth (and every other) Commandment!

Theologians and Bible scholars find no end of ingenious ways to dismiss as obsolete the marvelous laws of God. While most ministers will admit that keeping the Ten Commandments is generally "a good idea," they stress that they are not *required* in the New Testament for one to receive salvation. So there are other questions about the Law of God that must be answered before this volume is complete...

The Ultimate What If...?

Now we consider the greatest question of all: What if the whole world kept *all* the Ten Commandments? What if *everyone* obeyed Christ's instruction to keep this entire law?

People would no longer idolize anything or anyone, because they would put God first in their lives. God's name would no longer be misused or carelessly thrown around. Everyone would keep the Sabbath on the seventh day of the week. Families would be happier because people would honor their physical parents and their spiritual Father. There would be no more hatred, killing or war. Husbands and wives would be faithful to each other, and there would be no more illegitimate births. There would be no more sexually transmitted diseases. There would be no more thefts, robberies or embezzlements. Slander, perjury, and gossip would be things of the past. People would not lust for anything that belongs to someone else.

In Matthew 24, Christ described conditions that would precede His Second Coming. Verse 12 describes how "iniquity [Greek: lawlessness] shall abound" and the result would be that "the love of many shall wax cold."

But the time is coming when the whole world will keep God's Law—the Ten Commandments.

Does the
New Testament Teach
All Ten Commandments?

Now that we have examined, in some detail, each of the Ten Commandments, their spiritual application, and how radically different—and better!—the world would be if mankind obeyed them, we must ask: What about the New Testament: does it teach—and contain—all ten of God's commandments?

Most who profess to follow Christ believe the Ten Commandments were abolished by Jesus' sacrifice. They believe that Jesus came to "do away" with those "harsh" commandments. Some believe He re-instituted *some* of them. Still others believe that He replaced the Ten Commandments with a *new commandment* or commandments.

Although these people may be sincere, they have been deceived by the "god of this world" (II Cor. 4:4; Rev. 12:9), who has used his false ministers to spoon-feed them with doctrinal falsehood (II Cor. 11:13-15).

Instead of allowing the Bible to interpret itself, most people read into Scripture whatever meaning they already have been handed and assume is correct. They gloss over what Christ said in Matthew 5: "Think not that I am come to destroy the law, or the prophets: I am come not to destroy, but to fulfill" (vs. 17). This is the same Christ who prophesied in Isaiah 42: "The LORD is well pleased for His righteousness' sake; He will *magnify the law*, and make it honorable" (vs. 21).

What about you? Are you willing to let the Bible interpret itself? Are you willing to approach scripture with a teachable, open mind and allow God to "speak" to you—tell you His will—through His Word?

If so, you have already set yourself apart from most "believers," of whom Christ said, "This people honor Me with their lips, but their heart is far from Me. Howbeit in vain do they worship Me, teaching for doctrines the commandments of men. For laying aside the commandment of God, you hold the tradition of men...*Full well you reject the commandment of God*, that you may keep your own tradition" (Mark 7:6-9).

On Pentecost, A.D. 31, God founded His Church on the teachings of His apostles and prophets (Eph. 2:19-20). Since then, those of the true Church have always continued to keep the apostles' teachings (Acts 2:42).

The apostles Peter and John instructed Christians to walk as Christ walked—live the way He lived (I Peter 2:21; I John 2:6). The apostle Paul instructed Christians—both Jews *and* Gentiles—to follow him as he followed Christ (I Cor. 11:1).

So then, did Jesus Christ, the Chief Apostle (Heb. 3:1), teach the Ten Commandments? Did He command His apostles to do the same? In other words, are *all* of the Ten Commandments taught in the New Testament?

The First Great Commandment

We have seen that the first four of the Ten Commandments teach man how to love God. "You shall have no other gods before Me. You shall not make unto you any graven image...You shall not take the name of the LORD your God in vain...Remember the Sabbath day, to keep it holy" (Ex. 20:3-8).

In Matthew 22, Christ summarized these four, saying, "You shall love the LORD your God with all your heart, and with all your soul, and with all your mind. *This is the first and great commandment*" (vs. 37-38).

When Satan the devil tried to tempt Him while He fasted in the wilderness, Christ quoted the FIRST COMMANDMENT: "Get you behind Me, Satan: for it is written, *You shall worship the Lord your God*, and *Him only shall you serve*" (Luke 4:8; Matt. 4:10).

Recall in John 4:24, Christ was speaking about the SECOND COMMANDMENT when He taught that men cannot use physical objects, images or "aids"—in other words, idols—to worship a spiritual God. Since God is a Spirit, His followers must worship Him in spirit.

Paul taught the Second Commandment, too. "Neither be you *idolaters*, as were some of them [the Israelites during the Exodus]; as it is written, The people sat down to eat and drink, and rose up to play" (I Cor. 10:7). The context plainly establishes what Paul references. Carnal-minded Israel did not have the patience to worship a God they could not see, so they made a physical "god" to satisfy their carnal, physical lusts. But God knew this would happen. Throughout mankind's history, man has always rejected his Creator in order to worship His creation (Rom. 1:18-25).

In Matthew 15, Christ Himself taught against breaking the commandments by naming several, including indirectly referencing the third: "For out of the heart proceed evil thoughts, murders [SIXTH COMMANDMENT], adulteries [SEVENTH COMMANDMENT], fornications, thefts [EIGHTH COMMANDMENT], false witness [NINTH COMMANDMENT], *blasphemies* [THIRD COMMANDMENT]" (vs. 18-19). The Greek word used here for "blasphemies" is *blesphemia*, which means "evil speaking," "railing" or "vilification against God." In other words, taking God's name in vain.

Paul also commanded Christians not to do this. "But now you also put off all these; anger, wrath, malice, *blasphemy*, filthy communication out of your mouth" (Col. 3:8).

The FOURTH COMMANDMENT—observing the seventh day Sabbath—is the one most professing Christians refuse to obey. Most assume that men have the authority to change the Sabbath to whatever day pleases them or is convenient.

Yet Christ kept the Sabbath on the seventh day. This was His *custom*: "And He came to Nazareth, where He had been brought up: and, *as His custom was, He went into the synagogue on the Sabbath day*, and stood up for to read" (Luke 4:16). In fact, the New Testament records that Christ is "Lord also of the Sabbath"—not the Lord of Sunday (Luke 6:5). Christ states that He "is the same yesterday, and today, and forever" (Heb. 13:8).

Paul followed His example. He taught in the synagogues on the Sabbath (Acts 17:2). And not just to the Jews, but also to the Gentiles. "And when the Jews were gone out of the synagogue, the Gentiles besought that these words might be preached to them the *next Sabbath*... And the next Sabbath day came almost the whole city together to hear the word of God." (Acts 13:42, 44). In chapter 18, verse 4, Paul "reasoned in the synagogue *every Sabbath*, and persuaded the Jews *and the Greeks*." Few ask why Paul would teach Gentiles (who were unfamiliar with Sabbath-keeping) to meet on the Sabbath. Why is there no evidence that he led them to keep Sunday—the supposed "Lord's Day?"

Now notice Hebrews 4, verse 9: "There remains therefore a *rest* to the people of God." In verses 1, 3, 4 and 8, the Greek word for "rest" is *katapausin*. It means "rest." But in verse 9, the Greek word for "rest" is *sabbatismos*, which is a Hebrew word—*Sabbat*, which means "the Sabbath"—combined with a Greek suffix—*ismos*, which means "a keeping of" or "a doing of." Put together, *sabbatismo* means "a keeping of the Sabbath." When correctly translated, Hebrews 4:9 should read, "There remains therefore a *keeping of the Sabbath* to the people of God."

The subject of Sabbath-keeping requires a large book to contain all the available proof, but New Testament observance of the seventh-day Sabbath is established in Hebrews 4:9. (You are urged to read our book *Saturday or Sunday – Which Is the Sabbath?*)

The Second Great Commandment

We have seen the last six of the Ten Commandments instruct man how to love his fellow man. "Honor your father and your mother… You shall not kill. You shall not commit adultery. You shall not steal. You shall not bear false witness against your neighbor. You shall not covet…" (Ex. 20:12-17).

Centuries later, in the New Testament, in a context similar to Matthew 15, Christ said that anyone who wants to enter eternal life must keep these *same* commandments: "You shall do no murder [SIXTH COMMANDMENT], You shall not commit adultery [SEVENTH COMMANDMENT], You shall not steal [EIGHTH COMMANDMENT], You shall not bear false witness [NINTH COMMANDMENT], Honor your father and your mother [FIFTH COMMANDMENT]" (Matt. 19:18-19). Christ summarized these as "You shall love your neighbor as yourself," the second greatest commandment (Matt. 22:39).

Years after Christ's sacrifice (which most religious leaders claim does away with the law), Paul taught these same commandments to Gentile converts in Rome. "For this, You shall not commit adultery, You shall not kill, You shall not steal, You shall not bear false witness, You shall not covet; and if there be any other commandment, it is briefly comprehended in this saying, namely, You shall love your neighbor as yourself" (Rom. 13:9).

In Ephesians 6:2, Paul commanded Christians to obey the Fifth Commandment by honoring their parents. He commanded them to obey the Ninth Commandment: "Wherefore putting away lying, speak every man truth with his neighbor" (Eph. 4:25). He observed the Tenth Commandment, saying, "I had not known sin, but by the law: for I had not known lust, except the law had said, You shall not covet" (Rom. 7:7).

The apostle James also warned about the dangers of breaking the Tenth Commandment. "But every man is tempted, when he is drawn away of his own *lust*, and enticed. Then when lust has conceived, it brings forth sin: and sin, when it is finished, brings forth death" (1:14-15). He continued in chapter 4:

"From where come wars and fightings among you? Come they not hence, even of your *lusts* that war in your members? You lust, and have not: you kill, and desire to have, and cannot obtain: you fight and war, yet you have not, because you ask not. You ask, and receive not, because you ask amiss, that you may consume it upon your *lusts*" (vs. 1-3).

As you can see, *all* of the Ten Commandments were preached throughout the New Testament.

No wonder we saw that the apostle John wrote, "By this we know that we love the children of God, when we love God, and *keep His commandments*. For this is the love of God, *that we keep His commandments*: and His commandments are not grievous" (I John 5:2-3).

A New Commandment?

After examining all these biblical proofs, some will still believe that the Ten Commandments were abolished, refusing to give up what they have always assumed. They may even claim that the Ten Commandments were "replaced" by the "new commandment" Christ and John had taught. But what is this "new commandment"? Does it supersede keeping the Ten Commandments?

In John 13:34-35, Christ said, "A new commandment I give unto you, *That you love one another; as I have loved you, that you also love one another.* By this shall all men know that you are My disciples, if you have love one to another."

In Matthew 22:37-39, Christ said we must love our neighbors as ourselves. But in John 13, Christ gives a new and higher standard—to love others *as Christ loves us!* Only those with God's Holy Spirit dwelling in them can love people the way Christ does. "Because the carnal mind is enmity [hostile] against God: for it is not subject to the law of God, neither indeed can be. So then they that are in the flesh cannot please God. But you are not in the flesh, but in the Spirit, *if so be that the Spirit of God dwell in you.* Now if any man have not the Spirit of Christ, he is none of his...For as many as are *led by the Spirit of God, they are the sons of God"* (Rom. 8:7-9, 14).

This is talking about true Christians—those of GOD'S CHURCH!

When Christ said, "love one another, as I have loved you," He was talking to His disciples. They, later on, were baptized and received the Holy Spirit (see Acts 2), becoming the New Testament Church. Only true Christians—those with the Spirit of God in their minds—can hope to love others as Christ does. Carnal man cannot.

But what about the "new commandment" in I John 2:8? "Again, a new commandment I write unto you, *which thing is true in Him and in you*: because the darkness is past, and the true light now shines." What is it that is both "true in Christ" and "in" Christians?

The answer is in John 16:13-15, where Christ encouraged His disciples on the eve of His crucifixion. "Howbeit when [it], the *Spirit of truth*, is come, [it] will guide you into all truth: for [it] shall not speak of [itself]; but whatsoever [it] shall hear, that shall [it] speak: and [it] will show you things to come. [It] shall glorify Me: for [it] shall receive of Mine, and shall show it unto you. All things that the Father has are Mine: therefore said I, that [it] shall take of Mine, and shall show it unto you."

It is the Holy Spirit—the "Spirit of truth"—that is "true in Christ," and in His servants, members of His Church. This same spirit sets God's people apart from the world, converting their minds into the mind of Christ. The Holy Spirit empowers a Christian's mind, enabling it to love the way Christ and God the Father do. Without it, no human being can perfectly fulfill I Corinthians 13: "Love suffers long, and is kind; love envies not; love vaunts not itself, is not puffed up, does not behave itself unseemly, seeks not her own, is not easily provoked, thinks no evil; rejoices not in iniquity, but rejoices in the truth; bears all things, believes all things, hopes all things, endures all things. *Love never fails*" (vs. 4-8).

In II John 5-6, John wrote, "And now I beseech you, lady, not as though I wrote a new commandment unto you, *but that which we had from the beginning*, that we love one another. And this is love, *that we walk after His commandments*. This is the commandment, That, *as you have heard from the beginning*, you should walk in it." This scripture does not replace or do away with the Ten Commandments. Instead, it *reinforces* them!

The Ten Commandments existed before Moses from the time of Creation. All ten were taught throughout the New Testament. They are still in effect today.

Freed From "Everything?"

Even after examining all we have read so far, some readers (hopefully, only a tiny few) will still insist that keeping God's Law is "unnecessary." Some will argue Christians are freed from *everything* God commanded under the Old Covenant because Christ's sacrifice did away with it.

But did it?

Are Christians Freed From the Old Covenant?

M any professing Christians are confused about what Christ's sacrifice actually did away with, and what God requires of His people today. Many view the Old Covenant this way: If priestly duties, such as ceremonial washings, animal sacrifices, etc., are done away, then so is *everything* that God commanded under the Old Covenant. The following letter excerpts received at our Headquarters show the need to properly understand this subject:

"You probably will notice the emphasis of the book [of Leviticus] is on the ceremonies and rituals that God commanded of the Israelites. The book...seems to be a book documenting ceremonies and rituals; it basically explains the whole sacrificial system that the Israelites were commanded to perform, daily, weekly, monthly, annually, every seven years and every 50 years. Take note of what is part of that sacrificial system: Instructions regarding offerings, rules for ritual clean/unclean situations, instructions for the priesthood, tithing associated with the sacrificial system, association with the Sabbath and annual Holy Days.

"It is interesting that no church group has made any effort to explain how we could cease most or all of the practices of virtually all of 26 chapters of this book and yet maintain that we must keep 'parts' (but not all) of chapter 23. Is there an understanding that we can glean from this book that is consistent with scripture in the rest of the Bible?

"The book of Leviticus is an intriguing book that provides extensive guidelines about the sacrificial system as practiced by the Israelites and by the Jews in Jesus' time. But why do churches carefully ignore or misunderstand most, if not all, of its message? Have we even gotten the message right?

"This book does seem to present many of the 'practices' of the Israelites resulting from the covenant agreement that the Israelites made with God. An interesting question to consider: Does everything that this book teaches cease as a result of the sacrifice of Jesus Christ? Or just how much has ceased? Why has anything or all of the commands ceased? Is the sacrificial system outlined in this book to be considered as a package?"

Another person wrote, "Could you tell me if the health and other statutes in the Old Testament are still binding? We hear a lot about the Ten Commandments and Feasts, but hardly anything on these."

Why Such Confusion?

The core of these questions is this: How can something that was required of ancient Israel, and defined in excruciating detail, no longer be binding, while *other* requirements are still valid today? And what are those requirements? This confusion stems from misunderstanding the relevance today of the many laws given to ancient Israel. To understand, we must first define the term *civil law*.

A civil law is any mandate, law, decree or code regulating conduct and activity within the defined jurisdiction of an established municipality. The civil laws God gave to ancient Israel, through Moses, are presented in the books of Exodus, Leviticus and Deuteronomy. They reveal how to apply the principles set forth in the Ten Commandments. Together, the commandments, civil laws and statutes, and sacrificial laws comprise the Old Covenant.

We will examine some of the civil laws that governed ancient Israel, and show how they apply in the lives of Christians today, according to the *principles* Christ established in the New Testament.

Other than tithing and the observance of the Holy Days and the weekly Sabbath, what was required of ancient Israel, and adhered to by the Jews of Christ's day, that Christians must still practice today? To properly understand this issue, we must recognize a few basic principles, some repeated from earlier:

☐ (1) Israel was a physical, carnal-minded nation, without God's Holy Spirit. They were not offered eternal salvation. Many places in the Old Testament refer to them as the "*congregation* of Israel." Acts 7:38 refers to Israel as the "*church* in the wilderness." These terms mean the same thing. God chose them to be a *physical* "type" of His New Testament Church (those begotten of His Holy Spirit).

Notice I Corinthians 10:6: "Now these things [Israel's experiences] were *our examples*, to the intent we should not lust after evil things, as they also lusted." Their slavery in Egypt, deliverance under the leadership of Moses, crossing of the Red Sea and wandering in the wilderness were recorded in God's Word so that we can learn from their experiences.

Without God's Spirit, Israel could not properly keep God's *spiritual* laws (notice Romans 8:8). God gave them a long list of specific "do's and don'ts" because they could not keep the spirit of the Law. The Israelites *could not* obey God "in Spirit and in truth" (John 4:23-24). Because this was *impossible*, they had to have things spelled out in extra detail.

Fruit Hebrews 11:6 shows that it is impossible to please God without faith—and true faith is both a *fruit* (Gal. 5:22) and a *gift* (I Cor. 12:9) of the Holy Spirit. Only by receiving the Holy Spirit—"circumcision of the heart"—can one become a "spiritual Jew" (Rom. 2:28-29).

☐ (2) Israel was established as a union of church and state (Ex. 19:6; Acts 7:38), with detailed laws governing both their civil *and* religious matters. Ancient Israel was actually the Old Testament Church.

Critics of the Bible attempt to prove that God's Word is contradictory, and therefore invalid, by pointing to Malachi 3:6. There, Christ, the Rock of the Old Testament (I Cor. 10:1-5), stated, "For I am the LORD, I change not."

Such critics argue, "How can the Bible be valid as the Word of God if things *changed* between the Old Covenant and New Testament?"

The answer is simple: Think of God's Word as a contract between God and His people. The Old Covenant was essentially a marriage contract. The terms of the contract never change. But the terms cease to be in effect *between those two parties* if *either* party defaults—fails to keep his end of the bargain. The contract would have been broken. The *terms* of the contract would not change. But, within those terms are built-in "annulment" provisions.

Notice Hebrews 8:8: "For finding fault with *them* [ancient Israel and Judah], He says, Behold, the days come, says the Lord, when I will make a *new covenant* with the house of Israel and with the house of Judah." To understand, consider the following: "And all that dwell upon the earth shall worship [the beast], whose names are not written in the book of life of the Lamb *slain from the foundation of the world*" (Rev. 13:8).

God knew well in advance of man's creation that he would be capable of sinning. Adam was a free moral agent. He was given the *choice* of either obeying or rejecting God's laws. He could have chosen *not* to eat of the tree of the knowledge of good and evil, and rather to eat of the Tree of Life.

But Adam made the *wrong* choice. It was not at that point that God decided, "Oops! I didn't think of *that*. I've got to come up with something to pay for it! I guess I am going to have to send My Son as the sacrifice for sin." God knew that, even if Adam had made the right choice, *someone* would have eventually made the wrong choice.

The only mention God makes of something happening that was not part of His pre-ordained Plan was Israel's sacrificing of their children to pagan gods: "They have built also the high places of Baal, to burn their sons with fire for burnt offerings unto Baal, which I commanded not, nor spoke it, *neither came it into My mind*" (Jer. 19:5). This does not mean that God was taken off-guard. In His eyes, sin is sin (notice James 2:10-11). Israel was committing acts of murder as part of ceremonies for worshipping pagan gods. As horrific as this was, it did not require God to *re-think* His Plan.

When Paul states, in Galatians 3:19, "It [the body of law governing sacrifices] was added because of transgressions," he is referring to a "contractual provision," one that would *not* have been put into effect had Israel obeyed God. How do we know this? Notice Hosea 6:6: "For I [the Eternal] desired mercy, and *not sacrifice*; and the knowledge of God *more than burnt offerings*." (Also notice Psalm 40:6, 8.)

But animal sacrifices were not instituted by God as an *afterthought*, anymore than was Christ's sacrifice.

Christ Married Ancient Israel

The Old Covenant agreement between Christ and ancient Israel was actually a marriage *agreement*, or *covenant*. In Jeremiah 3:14, God said to Israel, "I am *married* unto you." Though He did later divorce her (3:8) for unfaithfulness, the marriage remained binding until Christ's death. Christ's marriage to, and divorce from, ancient Israel followed Old Testament law—see Ezekiel 16:38 and Deuteronomy 24:1.

Just as the Old Covenant was an agreement between God and *physical* Israel, the New Covenant is an agreement between God and *spiritual* Israel—true Christians today. But does this mean that the civil laws given to ancient Israel are no longer *binding* on Christians today?

To begin understanding this subject, we must first see what changed as a result of Christ's sacrifice:

(1) The need for animal sacrifices was eliminated (Heb. 9:12-14). Animal sacrifices pointed to *Christ's coming sacrifice.* They served to teach ancient Israel, in a graphic way, the penalty for sin—death. Once Christ came, offering Himself as the sacrifice for *all of mankind's* sins, there was no longer a need for the physical reminder.

(2) The *physical* duties of a *physical* high priest were replaced with the *spiritual* role of a *spiritual* High Priest—Christ (notice verse 11).

(3) Adhering to the strict letter of the Law was replaced with obeying both the spirit *and* letter of the Law. We will examine what this means for Christians today.

In other literature, we show that tithing, keeping the Sabbath and Holy Days, and obeying the Ten Commandments did not *originate* as part of the agreement (covenant means "agreement") that God made with Israel. The Old Testament reveals that God's servants understood and obeyed His laws long before they were given to Israel at Mount Sinai. (This was covered in Chapter One, and is found in our booklets *End All Your Financial Worries* and *God's Holy Days or Pagan Holidays? The* book *Saturday or Sunday – Which Is the Sabbath?* will also be helpful.)

A Misunderstood Scripture

Those who believe that Christ kept the Law for us (in our stead), and that all the requirements under the Old Covenant were "nailed to the cross," commonly cite Galatians 3:10-13. There, Paul wrote, "For as many as are of the *works of the law* are under the curse: for it is written, *Cursed is everyone that continues not in all things which are written in the book of the law to do them.* But that no man is *justified* by the law in the sight of God, it is evident: for, The just shall live by faith. And the law is not of faith: but, The man that does them shall live in them. Christ has *redeemed* us from the curse of the law, being made a curse for us: for it is written, *Cursed is everyone that hangs on a tree.*"

Many who read this scripture conclude that the Law itself is the curse and that Christ's sacrifice rendered it "null and void." But what did Paul really mean by "the curse of the law"? The answer is found in Hosea 13:14. There, Christ—the God of the Old Testament—said, "I will ransom them from the power of the grave; *I will redeem them from death*: O death, I will be your plagues; O grave, I will be your destruction: repentance shall be hid from Mine eyes."

What is the curse that Christ redeems us from? The death penalty!

But how did we incur this penalty? Notice: "Whosoever commits sin transgresses also the law: for *sin is the transgression of the law*" (I John 3:4)—"The soul that sins, *it shall die*" (Ezek. 18:4, 20)—"The wages of sin is *death*" (Rom. 6:23).

Also notice Romans 3:23: "For *all have sinned*, and come short of the glory of God." These scriptures (which we have addressed earlier in the book) show that Christ did not come to Earth as a physical human being, live a sinless life, and suffer a horrible, excruciating, humiliating death so that we would not have to keep God's laws.

What *was* Christ's purpose? He set the example for all true Christians to follow: "For even hereunto were you called: because Christ also suffered for us, *leaving us an example*, that you should *follow His steps*" (I Pet. 2:21).

Also notice Hebrews 2:10: "For it became Him [Christ], for whom are all things, and by whom are all things, in bringing many sons unto glory, to make the captain of their salvation perfect through sufferings." Christ died so that all mankind would have the opportunity for salvation.

Christ did not do away with the book(s) of the Law. Those who misinterpret Paul's words in Galatians 3 decide for themselves, "I can't possibly continue in *all things*, so to avoid being *cursed*, I must not be bound to *anything*." Many take an "all or nothing" or "pick and choose" approach to Christianity, arbitrarily deciding for themselves which of God's laws apply to *them*. This is perhaps most seen in the example of the Sabbath command.

Understanding the New Covenant

Hebrews 8:10 reveals that, through the New Covenant, God would put His laws "into [our] mind, and write them in [our] hearts." By receiving His Holy Spirit, Christians are able to keep His Law "in Spirit and in truth." Understand. The New Covenant has to do with people *obeying God*.

For example, notice Genesis 17:10. There, Christ commanded the patriarch Abraham, "Every man child among you shall be *circumcised*." As an outward *physical* sign between God and the *physical* nation of Israel, God required physical circumcision for those who obeyed Him in Old Testament times. The mandate under the Old Covenant was explicit: "And he that is *eight days old* shall be circumcised among you, every man child in your generations...And the uncircumcised man child whose flesh of his foreskin is not circumcised, that soul shall be cut off from his people; he has broken My covenant" (Gen. 17:12, 14).

However, under the New Covenant, God is selecting and calling out from the world a *spiritual* nation of Israel—His Church. Upon baptism and conversion, these few are led by the power of His Holy Spirit.

Paul explains: "For he is not a Jew, which is one *outwardly*; neither is that circumcision, which is outward in the flesh: but he is a Jew, which is one inwardly; and *circumcision is that of the heart*, in the spirit" (Rom. 2:28-29).

Through receiving God's Spirit, one becomes "circumcised in the heart." Physical circumcision is no longer the sign for one who follows and obeys God—spiritual circumcision is! The custom of circumcision was merely a forerunner—a physical parallel—of what God really wanted and intended for all mankind—circumcision of the heart (Jer. 4:4; Deut. 10:16; 30:6).

Upon conversion, a person becomes spiritually "circumcised." Paul further explains to the Colossians: "And you are complete in Him [Christ], which is the head of all principality and power: in whom also you are circumcised with the *circumcision made without hands*, in putting off the body of the sins of the flesh by the circumcision of Christ" (2:10-11).

For this reason, the apostles taught that *physical* circumcision was an Old Covenant requirement that did not need to be kept by

New Testament Christians (see Acts 15:24, 28). The need for circumcision was not eliminated, but rather changed—from physical to *spiritual*.

Notice Galatians 5:2-3: "Behold, I Paul say unto you, that if you [become] *circumcised*, Christ shall profit you nothing. For I testify again to every man that [becomes] circumcised, that he is a debtor to do the whole law."

In other words, if a man *believes* that his salvation hinges on being circumcised (a *physical* matter), then, as Paul pointed out in Galatians 3:10, it would become a *curse* to him: "For as many as are of the works of the law are under the curse: for it is written, Cursed is every one that continues not in all things which are written in the book of the law to do them."

Relying on physical rituals renders the sacrifice of Christ "of no effect" (5:4).

Christianity is a way of life based on things that a person *can* control, in his own life. Now notice: "Christ has redeemed us from the curse of the law [the death penalty], being made a curse for us: for it is written, *Cursed is everyone that hangs on a tree*" (Gal. 3:13).

Being hung on a tree was part of the process by which Christ fulfilled His role as our prophesied Savior: "Who His own self [Christ] bare our sins in His own body *on the tree*, that we, being dead to sins, should live unto righteousness" (I Pet. 2:24).

And remember that Christ said, "Think not that I am come to destroy the law, or the prophets: I am not come to destroy, but to fulfill" (Matt. 5:17).

But being cursed on a tree, which Paul paraphrased from Deuteronomy 21:23, would only apply in a civil setting. God does not empower His Church today to carry out such governmental functions in a similar way.

Other Examples

God has given us His laws for our own good. However, keeping the physical *civil laws* and other statutes, required under the Old Covenant, does not save anyone—just as keeping them did not guarantee salvation to the ancient Israelites. They were not even *offered* salvation at that time. But those laws *are* still binding—to the degree of their relevance in each Christian's life.

Again, this is not something that is left up to each person to arbitrarily decide for himself. "Counting the cost"—a vital part of the conversion process (Luke 14:28)—involves, among other things, examining the various aspects of your life—family, career, interests, etc.—and asking the question, "What do I have to change/alter/eliminate to bring my ways into harmony with God's ways?" See Isaiah 55:8-9.

For instance, some of the laws address issues of agriculture, business, civil engineering, etc. Obviously, such mandates are only applicable to those who work in those occupations. They would not have a bearing on the *actions* of those not employed in such fields. But they would *impact* the "end-users."

What many today do not consider is that many such codes and regulations enforced by man's laws are based on these principles (whether lawmakers, engineers, etc., realize it or not). For example, certain building codes that God gave Israel required the construction of a low wall around accessible roofs (Deut. 22:8). To show proper consideration for his fellowman (Matt. 7:12; Mark 12:31), an engineer would have to incorporate such a feature into building designs.

Another New Testament application of a law established under the Old Covenant is seen in modern Western bankruptcy law. God's guidelines for this are found in Deuteronomy 15:1-2: "At the end of every seven years you shall make a *release*. And this is the manner of the release: *Every creditor that lends ought unto his neighbor, shall release it*; he shall not exact it of his neighbor, or of his brother; because it is called the LORD's release."

To further understand the relevance today of the civil laws given to ancient Israel, notice what Paul wrote in I Corinthians 5:1: "It is reported commonly that there is fornication among you, and such fornication as is not so much as named among the Gentiles, *that one should have his father's wife*" (vs. 1). Where is this first mentioned? Notice Leviticus 20:11: "And the man that lies with his father's wife [in other words, his stepmother] has uncovered his father's nakedness: *both of them shall surely be put to death*; their blood shall be upon them."

Again, God's Church—spiritual Israel—is not empowered with the civil authority to exact the death penalty for sin. How then are we to address such problems? Consider: "I [Paul] wrote unto you in an epistle not to [keep] company with fornicators…if any man that is called a brother be a fornicator…with such an one no not to eat" (I Cor. 5:9, 11).

Obviously, that law is still binding today. But those who break it are not put to death. Rather, we are commanded to "*put away from among yourselves that wicked person*" (vs. 13).

Why? "To deliver such an one unto Satan for the destruction of the flesh, that the spirit may be saved in the day of the Lord Jesus" (vs. 5). The law itself was not changed—only the *application* of it!

The Conclusion of the Whole Matter

The Bible shows that in the Old Testament, God chose the physical nation of Israel to be His people, to set the example for other nations to see and follow. But, as we have seen, they failed to be that exemplary nation.

Today, God is calling people from many different physical nationalities to become "spiritual Israelites" (again read Romans 2:28-29).

Now notice His promise to ancient Israel: "A new heart also will I give you, and a new spirit will I put within you: and I will take away the stony heart out of your flesh, and I will give you an heart of flesh. And I will put My Spirit within you, and cause you to walk in My statutes, and you shall keep My judgments, and do them. And you shall dwell in the land that I gave to your fathers; and you shall be my people, and I will be your God" (Ezek. 36:26-28).

This will happen in the near future, beginning at Christ's Return!

Again, let's review Jeremiah 31:31-33: "Behold, the days come, says the LORD, that I will make a *new covenant* with the house of Israel, and with the house of Judah: not according to the covenant that I made with their fathers in the day that I took them by the hand to bring them out of the land of Egypt; which My covenant they broke, although I was an husband unto them, says the LORD.

"But this shall be the covenant that I will make with the house of Israel; after those days, says the LORD, I will put My law in their inner parts, and write it in their hearts; and will be their God, and they shall be My people."

How do we know that this has not happened yet?

Verse 34 provides the answer: "And they shall teach no more every man his neighbor, and every man his brother, saying, Know the LORD: *for they shall all know Me*, from the least of them unto the greatest of them, says the LORD: for I will forgive their iniquity, and I will remember their sin no more."

We can see that this is not happening now, in today's world—just as we can see that the fulfillment of Isaiah 2:4 will take place during the Millennium:

"And He [Christ] shall judge among the nations, and shall rebuke many people: and they shall beat their swords into plowshares, and their spears into pruninghooks: nation shall not lift up sword against nation, neither shall they learn war anymore."

Speaking of that future time, Christ says, "As for Me, this is My covenant with them, says the LORD; My Spirit that is upon you, and My words which I have put in your mouth, shall not depart out of your mouth, nor out of the mouth of your seed, nor out of the mouth of your seed's seed, says the LORD, from henceforth and for ever" (59:21).

This is the hope God has given us—*through* the New Covenant!

What Does the New Testament Teach About Law and Grace?

After all we have read thus far, we have come to understand the importance—and awesome significance—of faithfully observing God's commandments. We have come to recognize that God's Law is "holy, and the commandment holy, and just, and good" (Rom. 7:12), as well as *spiritual* (vs. 14), and has been in effect long before Moses. We have also proven that all Ten Commandments are taught in the New Testament, and that God expects man to live by them.

We now must ask another question: *What is the New Testament teaching on "law and grace"?* Is it one or the other—law *versus* grace—or both—law *and* grace?

This is a subject of great controversy, leaving many confused. *This need not be.* Here is the plain Bible teaching!

The meaning of grace in the New Testament has nothing to do with abolishing God's laws. False teachers who promote "grace" over obedience are unaware that the New Testament was written for those whom God calls to assume roles of great responsibility in His kingdom. These false teachers misunderstand because God has neither opened their minds nor given them His Holy Spirit, which is necessary to comprehend His truth.

The Christian calling (Rom. 8:29-30) is based on grace—*unmerited pardon of past sins* and *forgiveness* upon genuine repentance. Christians understand that the very salvation offered to them is a *gift*, and that they must continue to live a lifetime of obedience (Acts 5:32, John 14:15) and overcoming.

The Law in Perspective

Most religionists believe mankind is no longer burdened by the stringent requirements of that "harsh law" that stands in their way of freedom—of "having a good time." But we saw Paul wrote, in Romans 7:7, "What shall we say then? Is the law sin? God forbid. No, I had not known sin, *but by the law*: for I had not known lust, except the law had said, You shall not covet." Most churchmen have traditionally condemned the law while absolving sin. However, it is not the *law* that is at fault, but *sin*. On our own, we cannot discover God's perfect law. God has to reveal and teach it to us.

Leaders of professing Christianity insist that God's spiritual law—the Ten Commandments—is done away. They call it the "law of Moses," claiming that it was abolished by Christ's sacrifice. But they do not know the difference between the Levitical sacrificial rituals, the law of Moses and the law of God.

The Ten Commandments were not called the law of Moses, but rather the *law of God*. The law of Moses consisted of: (1) the civil laws—the statutes and judgments that Moses relayed to the people from God, recorded in Exodus 21-23 and the remaining books of the Law—and (2) the ritualistic laws (Greek: *ergon*) added later, summarized in Hebrews 9:10. These ordinances regulated the Levitical sacrifices (Lev. 1-7) and related duties. *Ergon* means "works," as in the "works of the law" (Gal. 2:16). This referred to the labor involving Levitical rituals abolished by Christ's sacrifice.

Remember, the Ten Commandments were never part of the law of Moses or the Levitical sacrificial system. The civil laws and sacrifices were based on God's Commandments, which make up the core of God's laws. Thus, the Ten Commandments precede and transcend every lesser law based upon them—statutes, judgments, precepts and ordinances. Most professing Christians falsely brand the Ten Commandments as the "Old Covenant." However, the Old Covenant was based on the Ten Commandments, which preceded and transcended the Old Covenant.

Consider an analogy: The idea promoted by most professing Christians—that the Ten Commandments have been abolished—is as ridiculous as claiming that the physical laws of gravity and inertia are no longer enforced. Theologians cannot negate God's Law any more than scientists can void the laws of gravity and inertia.

How did the leaders of the early Church view the laws of God? Paul wrote, "Wherefore the law is *holy*, and the commandment *holy, and just, and good*" (Rom. 7:12). Again, the apostle John wrote, "For *this is the love of God* that we *keep His commandments* and His commandments *are not grievous*" (I John 5:3)—no matter the opinion of "no law" teachers. And Christ summed up the matter, saying, "…if you will enter into life, *keep the commandments*" (Matt. 19:17).

In Matthew 7:21, He also said, "Not everyone that says unto Me, Lord, Lord, shall enter into the kingdom of heaven; but he that *does the will* of My Father which is in heaven"!

Christ and the apostles did not dismiss God's Law. Counterfeit Christianity took this drastic step in the first century—the world has blindly followed ever since.

The "Grace" of False Christianity

Let's examine traditional Christianity's teaching of grace. It teaches that the Old Covenant *was* the Ten Commandments. It maintains that Christ came to establish a "new covenant" containing only grace and promises—liberty to do whatever one pleases. Law is not included in their package. In their own minds, these creative religionists have devised a way to "have a good time" and have a clear conscience. They had to eliminate the source of their gnawing guilt. The solution was simple: "Grace alone 'saves' men. The burden of commandment-keeping is no longer necessary."

This diabolical teaching would lead you to believe that the law of God is harsh and cruel. It proclaims that the fault of the Old Covenant was with the *law*, and since God gave the law, the fault must have been *His*. Recall what Christ says to those who follow these false precepts: "Howbeit in vain do you worship Me, teaching for doctrines the commandments of men. For *laying aside the commandment of God*, you hold the tradition of men…Full well you *reject* the *commandment of God*, that you may keep your *own* tradition" (Mark 7:7-9).

Notice the warning that God inspired in the book of Jude: "Beloved, when I gave all diligence to write unto you of the common salvation, it was needful for me to write unto you, and exhort you that you should earnestly contend for the faith which was *once delivered* unto the saints. For there are certain men crept in unawares who were before of old ordained to this condemnation, ungodly men, turning the *grace* of our God into *lasciviousness*, and denying the only Lord God, and our Lord Jesus Christ" (Jude 3-4).

Even before the New Testament was completely written, ungodly men had crept into the Church in an attempt to corrupt it by turning *grace* into *lasciviousness*. This was precisely the false gospel taught by Simon Magus, Nicholas of Samaria, Cerinthus and other "founders" of counterfeit Christianity.

Lasciviousness means "license to sin." It could also be defined as "unrestrained liberty" or "abuse of privilege." In essence, this means doing what seems right in one's own eyes, according to one's own conscience.

Just as Simon Magus (Acts 8:9-24) and others turned God's grace into license to disobey His law, this same attitude permeates the minds of most professing Christians today.

The universal message from pulpits falsely tells people Christ abolished His Father's law—but the Bible states otherwise. No one can be born into God's kingdom unless he completely submits to God's authority.

Grace—the True Definition

Webster's New Collegiate Dictionary defines *grace* as "favor, kindness and mercy." The ecclesiastical usage is defined as "divine mercy and forgiveness." No mention is made about grace being license to disobey God's Law. To be "under grace" means to be extended *mercy* and *forgiveness* as a result of sincere repentance and resolve to obey God.

This is explained further in Romans 6:14-15: "For sin shall not have dominion over you for you are not *under the law*, but under grace. What then? *Shall we sin*, because we are not under the law, but under grace? *God forbid*." Many misunderstand the concept of "under the law," which simply means *under the penalty of the law*. Notice Galatians 5:18: "But if you are led by the Spirit, you are not under the law." You *are* under the penalty of the law if you violate it as a way of life.

But a person led by God's Spirit will strive to follow that law. When he occasionally sins, he repents and is forgiven (I John 1:8-10). By virtue of obedience and grace, he is not under the *penalty* of the law.

When an individual seeks to obey God and comes under the "umbrella" of grace, the blood of Christ justifies, or forgives, all past transgressions. Repentance shows God the direction a Christian chooses to take from that time forward. Having been made right with God by His mercy and forgiveness, a Christian embarks on a new course in life—he is *SAVED* by Christ's *LIFE*, not His death!

Consider! Only if Christ has risen from the dead can His Spirit guide and strengthen new converts, for it is the Holy Spirit that leads Christians.

This means that Jesus Christ, as our living, active High Priest in Heaven, sends the Holy Spirit to those whom the Father calls and begets. As High Priest, Christ is our living Intercessor and Advocate, who sees us through life as we seek to overcome and endure to the end. The fact that Christ is alive allows Him to function as an Advocate for Christians. In this way, we are saved by His life. Repentance is a continual state of mind. Thus, forgiveness is also continual. Also, it is the Spirit of the living Christ in Christians that will change them at the resurrection (Rom. 8:14-17), so that they can receive eternal life.

How Is One Saved?

Romans 6:23 explains that the wages of sin is death. Upon repentance, baptism and conversion, a Christian is forgiven by the blood of Christ and *immediately* saved from the penalty of *past* sins. So, in one sense, the person has been "saved," *at that moment*, from death.

There are two more applications of when and how a person is saved. The word s*alvation* is derived from the word *saved*. So, the second way is the most obvious—salvation at the resurrection upon Christ's Return (I Cor. 15:50-55; I Thes. 4:13-18).

The third way one is saved is that he is "being saved." No one receives salvation in this life without first undergoing much trial, testing, learning, growing and overcoming. Salvation is an *ongoing process*—throughout one's lifetime.

Notice what Paul wrote in Romans 5: "Much more then *being justified by His blood*, we shall be saved from wrath through Him. For if, when we were enemies, we were reconciled to God by the death of His Son, much more being reconciled, we shall *be saved by His life*" (vs. 9-10).

Salvation results from grace—unmerited pardon. The calling to and the gift of repentance are not earned by works. God's grace is not earned by works. All that human beings have earned is death. *However, to be under grace does not mean that we have already achieved salvation.* It means we have been given unmerited pardon and are in the lifelong process of overcoming and enduring. Those who endure to the end of this physical existence are saved—from what?—from eternal death.

No one can boast that he has achieved salvation in this life. "But he that shall *endure unto the end, the same shall be saved*" (Matt. 24:13; 10:22). Having endured and overcome means that one has "qualified." It also means that one can *disqualify* himself by failing to endure or overcome. Yet, the calling, the justification—*this* grace is a gift. Salvation results from God's grace.

The false idea that "once under grace, we are already saved" is not founded upon Scripture. Grace is God's willingness to forgive *past sins*, as summarized in Ephesians 1:7: "…in whom we have redemption through His blood, the forgiveness of sins, according to the riches of His grace."

Now examine a key scripture: "For by grace are you saved through faith; and that not of yourselves: it is the gift of God: not of works, lest any man should boast" (Eph. 2:8-9). The faith "not of yourselves," instrumental to salvation, *is not your own human* faith. It is the *gift of God*—the faith *of Christ* in us (Gal. 2:20). Jesus Christ, our High Priest, looks down and observes our sincerity and effort, and imparts His faith to us through His grace—divine favor and mercy. Those who receive this faith have no grounds for boasting of *their* works.

Notice the following: "…for it is GOD which works in you both to will and to do His good pleasure" (Phil. 2:13). God provides Christians with the *willpower, faith of Christ* and *motivation* to do His good pleasure. God the Father and Jesus Christ have gone to great lengths to provide the grace—favor and divine mercy—to help Christians succeed in their calling. But they expect *results*! That is the message of Ephesians 2: "For we are His workmanship, created in Christ Jesus *unto good works*, which God has before ordained that we should *walk in them*" (vs. 10).

How plain the Bible becomes when we let it interpret itself! It is ironic that most professing Christians stop at this point and miss the very core of Paul's statement.

The real issue here is not grace *or* works. Neither is it grace *opposed to* works. Nor is it grace *in the place of* works. It is simply this: grace *followed by* works.

Here are some vital gifts and tools that God gives in our quest to succeed and overcome:

- Grace—justification and forgiveness.
- Grace—God's giving of mercy and favor.
- The faith of Christ in us.
- God's Spirit, through which we receive the willpower and motivation to forge ahead.

God extends grace and help to His people, but He expects us to grow in good works, *walking in them* as a way of life. The law of God is the standard or benchmark that directs the paths of true Christians. Keeping them develops character. Doing these things shows God that the grace He has extended to us has not been in vain.

If we follow God's grace with works, Christ's description of those who will rise at the first resurrection could apply to us: "Here is the patience of the saints: *here are they that keep the commandments of God*, AND THE FAITH OF JESUS" (Rev. 14:12).

(This subject is covered in additional detail in my booklet *What Is Your Reward in the Next Life?*)

Does the New Testament Contain New Commandments?

In their zeal to get rid of the Ten Commandments, most professing Christians conclude that the New Testament's "new commandments" somehow abolished them. The Bible suggests nothing of the sort!

Christ declared in impossible to misunderstand terms, "Think not that I am come to destroy the law, or the prophets: I am *not come to destroy*, but to *fulfill*. For verily I say unto you, Till heaven and earth pass, one jot or one tittle shall in no wise pass from the law, till all be fulfilled. *Whosoever therefore shall break one of these least commandments*, and shall teach men so, he shall be called the *least* in the kingdom of heaven: but whosoever *shall do* and *teach* them, the same shall be called *great* in the kingdom of heaven" (Matt. 5:17-19).

The Greek word for "fulfill" is *pleroo*. Its meaning depends upon the context. In this case, the translators' use of the word "fulfill" correctly fits the context. They could have also used "satisfy," "complete" or "accomplish." For example, suppose the word "end" was used for *pleroo*. "End" would not fit the context, because the verse would read, "...I am not come to destroy, but to end." This would be meaningless—"end" and "destroy" mean the same thing!

Another key passage we saw is Matthew 19:17. Christ was asked a profound question by a wealthy nobleman: "Good Master, what good thing shall I do, that I may have eternal life?" Christ answered,

"Why call you Me good? There is none good but One, that is, God: but if you will enter into [eternal] life, *keep the commandments*."

Christ's New Commandment

Recall Christ stated, "A new commandment I give unto you, *That you love one another*; as I have loved you, that *you also love one another*. By this shall all men know that you are My disciples, if *you have love one to another*" (John 13:34-35). He also taught this in Matthew 22: "You shall love the Lord your God with all your heart, and with all your soul, and with all your mind. This is the first and great commandment. And the second is like unto it, *You shall love your neighbor as yourself*" (vs. 37-39).

There is no hint of God's Law being done away, suspended or replaced by "love" or any other religious sounding phrase.

In Matthew 22, the old standard was seen to be to love others as yourself. But in John 13, Christ gives us a new and higher standard— to love others as *He* loves us.

While the Ten Commandments were given to the nation of Israel as the basis of the covenant between the Israelites and God, they also apply to all humanity for all time. God revealed to the Israelite nation what He will ultimately reveal to every nation of the world. Israel was a carnal people, not yet given God's Spirit. Thus, they could only keep the *letter* of the law. This was the old version of "love toward neighbor."

The new version was given on the night before Christ was crucified. He instructed His disciples, who became the original apostles and leaders of His Church. This instruction applied to His Church.

Notice John 17:9, 11: "I pray for them: I pray not for the world, but for them which You have given Me; for they are Yours...and now I am no more in the world, but these are in the world, and I come to You. Holy Father, keep through Your own name those who You have given Me, that they may be one, as We are."

The older version—love toward your neighbor—is still in effect today. So are the Ten Commandments. The new command applies specifically to God's Church, not the world. The Church is the mother who nurtures those who are preparing for positions of responsibility in the kingdom of God.

God's Church has His Spirit and follows Christ's example (I Peter 2:21). Only with God's Holy Spirit can one keep this new commandment. To require someone without God's Spirit to love some-one as Christ loves him would be *unreasonable* and actually *impossible* (Rom. 5:5).

For people in the world, God considers loving your neighbor as yourself to be both reasonable and possible. When God's Spirit becomes available to all mankind, the standard will be raised. Take a moment to see in Ephesians 5:22-33 that this is already the case in marriages between those with God's Spirit.

New Commandment From John

Now read I John 2:7-9: "Brethren, I write no new commandment unto you, but an old commandment which you had from the beginning. The old commandment is the word which you have heard from the beginning. Again, a new commandment I write unto you, which thing is true in Him and in you: because the darkness is past, and the true light now shines. He that says he is in the light, and hates his brother, is in darkness even until now."

Notice that nothing is changed as far as the Ten Commandments are concerned. We saw proof of this in the previous chapter. Nothing is mentioned about doing away with it. Notice the phrase, "which thing is true in Him and in you." It followed the phrase, "Again, a new commandment I write unto you."

What is the thing that is "true in Christ" that is in you (brethren to whom John sent this letter)? Here is the answer: "Howbeit when it, the Spirit of truth, is come, it will guide you into all truth: for it shall not speak of itself; but whatsoever it shall hear, that shall it speak: and it will show you things to come. It shall glorify Me: for it shall receive of Mine, and shall show it unto you. All things that the Father has are Mine: therefore said I, that it shall take of Mine, and shall show it unto you" (John 16:13-15).

A careful reading of this passage reveals that it is the Holy Spirit, the Spirit of truth, that is what is "true in Christ." The Holy Spirit is in Christ, and in the members of the Church of God. It is His Spirit that sets His people apart from the world—this is the key message of I John 2:7-9.

In II John 5-6, John stated, "And now I beseech you, lady [a term from the New Testament], not as though I wrote a new commandment unto you, but that which we had from the beginning, that we love one another. And *this is love*, that we *walk after His command-*

ments. This is the commandment, That, as you have heard from the beginning, you should walk in it."

As before, this scripture does away with nothing. In fact, what John calls a new commandment still applies today. Notice the statement, "And this is love, that we walk after His commandments." (This is the same as what we saw in John's first epistle.)

Let's see again how Paul summed up God's wonderful, perfect Law: "Wherefore the law is holy, and the commandment holy, and just, and good" (Rom. 7:12). We must seek God so "That He may incline our hearts unto Him, to walk in all His ways, and to keep His commandments, and His statutes, and His judgments, which He commanded our fathers" (I Kings 8:58).

How the New Testament Defines Sin

The Bible states that you have at least one thing in common with every man, woman and child who has ever lived: *"For all have sinned, and come short of the glory of God"* (Rom. 3:23). God's Word also states that when (not if) you sin, you automatically *earn* the penalty of death (Rom. 6:23).

But what *is* sin—what have you *done* to earn death?

God declares that your sins separate you from Him (Isa. 59:1-2). This is serious; in fact what could be more serious? He cannot hear your prayers, He cannot speak to you through His Word, unless you first repent—change your life—from the way of sin!

But what *is* sin—what have you *done* to separate yourself from God? While this was covered briefly at the beginning of the book, it is now critical to take a detailed look at what the New Testament says about the topic.

When asked to define sin, most people stammer about, searching their thoughts for an answer, before falling back on the cliche, "Well, Christ died for our sins."

Yes, Jesus Christ did sacrifice His innocent, sinless life for the sins of mankind—but this does not tell us WHAT sin *is*!

When further pressed to give the biblical definition of sin, the same people will stick to their original answer: "Christ died for us!" Many simply cannot comprehend the question, nor do they understand that God's Word clearly defines sin.

Do not accept human interpretation or personal opinion! The *Bible's* definition of sin can be known to those with open minds, to all who truly *want* to know the mind of God!

When people say, "Christ saved us from our sins," shouldn't they—shouldn't you?—know *exactly* what is it that caused the death of an innocent, eternal God-being? To say "He died for sin" comes way short of understanding what Christ died for. Whatever it is, it must be very big, very SPECIFIC, to require the death of a divine Savior.

Even people who have never opened a Bible are familiar with John 3, verse 16: "For God so loved the world, that He gave His only begotten Son, that whosoever believes in Him should not perish, but have everlasting life." Most understand that God willingly allowed Jesus Christ to suffer arrest, false accusations, humiliation, and endure brutal torture and public execution—sacrifice—all so that His shed blood would pay the death penalty, which each of us have earned. In other words, Christ had to die because of the sins of all human beings—including you!

Once again, just what *is* sin—what have you *done* to sentence Christ to death?

When a leading American statesman was caught in a sex scandal, his defenders tried to excuse his actions. They paraphrased Christ, in John 8:7, saying, "He who is without sin, let him cast the first stone."

Actually, Jesus was speaking to the scribes and Pharisees, who had brought before Him a woman they had caught committing adultery. Testing Him, they wanted to see whether Christ would follow Old Testament law and condemn her to be stoned.

Most people who quote John 8:7 do so in order to justify wrong actions. But they fail to read the rest of the scripture: "And they [the scribes and Pharisees] which heard it, being convicted by their own conscience, went out one by one, beginning at the eldest, even unto the last: and Jesus was left alone, and the woman standing in the midst. When Jesus had lifted up Himself, and saw none but the woman, He said unto her, Woman, Where are those your accusers? Has no man condemned you? She said, No man, Lord. And Jesus said unto her, Neither do I condemn you: *go, and sin no more*" (vs. 9-11).

This is vital. Christ commanded her to *stop sinning*—but what did He mean?

The Bible Definition

Many religious leaders teach that Christ died for our sins. They teach that His shed blood *cleanses* us from sin. They preach about being set free from *bondage* to sin. But they also preach about freedom from keeping God's Law and have you noticed that they never define what sin *is*—that they never challenge people to look into their Bibles to see how *God* defines sin?

If they did, they would have to tell you to read I John 3:4, where the apostle John wrote, "Whosoever commits sin transgresses [breaks] also the law: for *sin is the transgression* [breaking] *of the law*." Do not miss this point! When you sin, you break the law!

When the Bible says, "For all have sinned," it means that everyone has *broken God's Law*. When it says, "the wages of sin is death," it means that your *lawbreaking* automatically earns you the death penalty. When God says that your sins separate you from Him, He's talking about you *breaking His law*. Sin is breaking God's law!

But what law?

The apostle Paul wrote, "What shall we say then? Is the law sin? God forbid. Nay, *I had not known sin, but by the law*" (Rom. 7:7). God's Law *reveals* sin.

But what law was Paul writing about? It is important to review the following passage in light of the chapter's title.

"...for I had not known lust, except the law had said, You shall not COVET" (same verse). This is the Tenth Commandment, found in Exodus 20:17 and Deuteronomy 5:21. The law that Paul and John referred to was the Ten Commandments. Both apostles taught that when you break these commandments, you *sin*.

John also wrote, in I John 5:17, "All *unrighteousness* is sin." Since God's commandments are righteousness (Psa. 119:172), then unrighteousness—sin!—*must* be the opposite. It is *breaking* God's commandments.

The apostle James expanded upon this. He taught that "whosoever shall keep the whole law, and yet *offend* [sin] in *one point*, he is guilty of *all*. For He that said, Do not commit adultery, said also, Do not kill. Now if you commit no adultery, yet if you kill, you are become a *transgressor of the law* [a lawbreaker]" (2:10-11). James was obviously referring to the Ten Commandments.

Even though it is possible for people to go through life without ever physically committing a murder or adultery, or stealing or lying, nevertheless, *all have sinned*. How can this be? Because although one can obey the *letter* of the law, he can still break the *spirit* of the law—and this is also sin.

Christ *magnified* and expanded the letter of the law, revealing its spiritual intent. "You have heard that it was said by them of old time, You shall not commit adultery: but I say unto you, That whosoever looks on a woman to *lust* after her has *committed adultery* with her already *in his heart*" (Matt. 5:27-28).

Always Starts in the Mind

Sin begins in the mind. What you *think* eventually becomes what you *do* (Prov. 23:7)! "But those things which proceed out of the mouth come forth from the heart [mind]; and they defile the man. For out of the heart proceed *evil thoughts*, murders, adulteries, fornications, thefts, false witness, blasphemies: These are the things which defile a man" (Matt. 15:18-20).

James 1:14-15 shows that when men entertain wrong *thoughts*, they will eventually produce wrong *actions*. "But every man is tempted, when he is drawn away of his own lust, and enticed. Then when lust has conceived, it brings forth sin: and sin, when it is finished, brings forth death [the wages of sin]."

For example, every war, every battle, every fight throughout history has happened because men have coveted something that did not belong to them. And because men have failed to control their carnal desires, we live in a world wracked by the pain, suffering and anguish of war (Jms. 4:1-2).

Example of Lust Conceiving Sin

The Bible records a tragic, historic example of how one man's lustful thoughts conceived sin—lawbreaking—and gave birth to death. That man was King David.

One spring evening, as David walked on the roof of his palace, he spotted a naked woman who was washing herself (II Sam. 11:2). Instead of looking away, and putting her image out of his mind, he stared at her. He allowed his mind to entertain wrong thoughts—and in so doing, David broke the Tenth Commandment.

This sin led him to ask about her (vs. 3). He discovered that she was Bathsheba, the wife of Uriah, one of his most trusted servants. But this did not stop David from committing adultery with her (vs. 4), breaking the Seventh Commandment. David also broke the Eighth Commandment by taking what did not belong to him—Uriah's wife.

These sins resulted in David and Bathsheba conceiving an illegitimate child (vs. 5). Wanting to cover up the pregnancy, David tried to deceive Uriah, who had been away, faithfully fighting a war for his king. Recalling him from the frontlines, David tried to deceive Uriah into sleeping with Bathsheba, so he would think the unborn child was his (vs. 6-13). These actions broke the principle of the Ninth Commandment.

When Uriah refused to sleep with her, David's growing mountain of sins led him to use his enemies to murder Uriah (vs. 14-17)—thus breaking the Sixth Commandment.

What had begun with evil thoughts soon led to multiple sins—lawbreaking—and eventually to murder. This is just one example of how sin always spreads. Every action—adultery, murder, stealing, among others, invariably requires at least the additional sin of lying to cover it up.

God Hates Sin—Lawbreaking

Eventually, David repented. He came to see his sins the way God saw them—as terrible lawbreaking—iniquity. That is why David wrote, in Psalm 5:4-5, "For You are not a God that has pleasure in wickedness: neither shall evil dwell with You. The foolish shall not stand in Your sight: You hate all workers of iniquity [sin]."

After God had freed the Israelites from slavery, fed, protected and provided for them, gave them the Promised Land, and fought their battles for them, they still continued to sin—to break His commandments. "Yet they tempted and provoked the Most High God, and kept not His testimonies: but turned back, and dealt unfaithfully like their fathers: they were turned aside like a deceitful bow. For they provoked Him to anger with their high places, and moved Him to jealousy with their graven images. When God heard this, He was wroth, and greatly *abhorred* Israel" (Psa. 78:56-59).

God cannot, will not ever, tolerate sin or those who practice it! He would never allow such people in His kingdom.

Solomon, David's son, wrote in Proverbs 15:26, "The thoughts of the wicked are an abomination to the LORD." This is because God knows that, if unchecked, wicked *thoughts* always produce wicked *actions*, as in Jeremiah 44: "So that the LORD could no longer bear, because of the *evil of your doings*, and because of the *abominations* which you have committed...because you have *sinned* against the LORD, and have *not obeyed* the voice of the LORD, *nor walked in His law*, nor in his statutes, nor in his testimonies..." (vs. 22-23).

Sin—breaking God's spiritual law—cuts us off from God. "But your *iniquities* have separated between you and your God, and your *sins* have hid His face from you, that he will not hear" (Isa. 59:2). And Jeremiah wrote, "Your iniquities have turned away these things, and your sins have withholden good things from you" (Jer. 5:25).

When God used His prophet, Nathan, to confront David, the king begged God to "Cast me not away from Your presence" (Psa. 51:11). He acknowledged his transgressions to God, saying, "My sin is ever before me. Against You, You only, have I sinned, and done this evil in Your sight: that You might be justified when You speak, and be clear when You judge" (vs. 3-4). David pleaded with God to "blot out my transgressions. Wash me thoroughly from mine iniquity, and cleanse me from my sin... Purge me with hyssop, and I shall be clean: wash me, and I shall be whiter than snow... Hide Your face from my sins, and blot out all mine iniquities. Create in me a clean heart, O God" (vs. 1-2, 7, 9-10).

God heard and forgave.

You Can Overcome and Prevent Sin

All who have been called to God's way of life have struggled against the pulls of the flesh and the temptations of Satan and his world. Some overcome. Others do not.

Christ said, "Enter you in at the *strait* [difficult] gate: for wide is the gate, and broad [easy] is the way, that leads to destruction, and *many* there be which go in thereat: because strait [difficult] is the gate, and *narrow* is the way, which leads unto life, and *few* there be that find it" (Matt. 7:13-14). Most seek the easy, "broad" path.

Overcoming is hard—difficult!—it is a life-long struggle. But it IS possible. You *can* overcome. If you are a Christian, you *must*!

Yet, this world is drifting along, completely unaware of God's marvelous purpose for man, which is to build character in this life. He is preparing a team of those who will qualify to be part of restoring His government to earth at Christ's Return.

The Bible Pattern

The Bible is filled with accounts of God's greatest servants battling to overcome sin. In nearly every case, they had to learn difficult, and sometimes painful, lessons. When examined collectively, Moses, Noah, David, Samuel, Peter and others are seen to have fought every kind of problem known to man. They battled sins, weaknesses, faults, attitudes, and pulls and temptations of the flesh. David fought sins and wrong attitudes and overcame them. Moses lacked faith and confidence and had a temper that he had to overcome. Yet, he will hold a high office in God's kingdom. Both Job and Elijah fought discouragement and depression, even to the point of wanting to die. But these men endured—they overcame. They slew their problems, rather than being slain by them!

These men were actively *trained* by God and had to OVERCOME Satan, the temptations of his world and the pulls of the flesh. A Christian is one who OVERCOMES his problems, weaknesses, sins and wrong attitudes, rather than being overcome and defeated *by* them!

To the Overcomer

Through John, Christ said, "And he that OVERCOMES, and keeps My works unto the end, to him will I give *power over the nations*: and he shall *rule them* with a rod of iron" (Rev. 2:26-27).

In His instruction to the *Laodicean* era of His Church, He adds, "To him that OVERCOMES will I grant to sit with Me in My throne, *even as I also overcame*, and am set down with My Father in His throne" (Rev. 3:21).

These verses picture Christ re-establishing God's government over all nations of the earth. Christians will receive REAL POWER to RULE. But first they must overcome.

Christians are those who follow—who copy—Christ (I Pet. 2:21). Then what is the pattern Christ established for us to follow? Did *He* overcome?

In reference to His own struggle to remain free of sin, perfect in character, Christ said, "In the world you shall have tribulation [how true!]: but be of good cheer; *I have overcome the world*" (John 16:33). Christ had overcome both the world and its god—Satan (II Cor. 4:4). Recall that Christ said, "EVEN AS I ALSO OVERCAME, and am set down with My Father in His throne." Jesus Christ overcame and qualified to rule. Just as He qualified to replace Satan, so must we!

Such enormous power to rule could never be given to people who are unprepared—who have not *qualified* to properly use it. God will not hand great authority to people who might rebel and revert to Satan's ways. God's servants must use this life to build His very character, so necessary for those holding offices of great authority.

Experienced in Sin

Understand! You have been practicing yielding to the flesh and Satan's way for your entire life. You have probably become *very good* at both. Believe me, as you strive to overcome and resist the pulls at work within you, you will find that wrong patterns of conduct are "second nature" to you—more than you now know! Left unchecked, human nature consists of vanity, jealousy, lust, greed, envy, resentment, hatred, anger, pride, rebellion, foolishness, deceit and hostility toward God. This is what you have been practicing—possibly for decades.

Overcoming will not be easy or happen overnight. It is a lifelong struggle against well-established attitudes and a former way of life that the Christian has now rejected and turned from. The one who is walking God's path is striving to curb and *withhold* himself wherever God's Word instructs. He strives to *exercise* himself in all matters where God says to do so. When God gives instruction to do something, he strives to do it! When God gives instruction *not* to do something, he strives *not* to do it!

Learning to do this takes a lifetime. But remember: Building character is why you were born. Your job is to "put off" the fleshly pulls of human nature, and to "put on" the character of God and Christ (Col. 3:8-13). Though this is not easy, the reward is great.

God looks on the intent of your heart. It is your overall desire and motivation that is important to Him. He wants to know if, after you sin, you are sorry for it and are determined to strive to do better. He understands the temptations that beset us even better than we do. He watches to see if we will be sober and vigilant as we root sin out of our lives. Will we carelessly fall back into old patterns? Will we try to overcome on human strength and energy?

God's Power at Conversion

We have seen that a Christian is led by the Holy Spirit of God (Rom. 8:9, 14). It enters at repentance and baptism (Acts 2:38). It is this Spirit in a converted mind that empowers one with the strength to change what human "steam" alone cannot. II Timothy 1:7 states, "For God has not given us the spirit of fear; but of POWER, and of love and of a sound mind."

The Greek word for power is *dunamis*. It means "special miraculous power or force." At conversion, you were literally given REAL POWER! This power builds up and establishes the righteousness of God within your character. You must draw upon the strength from God's Spirit on a daily basis to successfully overcome. This strength is unlimited and is sufficient to defeat any sin, problem or attitude—no matter how large and foreboding such may appear!

But make no mistake! We must not build our *own righteousness*. This does not impress God. He sees it as so many "filthy rags" (Isa. 64:6). Paul wrote of his own personal hope, as a Christian, to "be found in Him, *not having Mine own righteousness*, which is of the law, but that which is *through the faith of Christ*, the righteousness which is of God by faith" (Phil. 3:9).

The Role of Faith

Exactly what role does faith play in overcoming—in growth? It does play a role, but how?

Ephesians 2:8-9 states, "For by grace are you saved *through faith*; and that [the faith] not of yourselves: it is the gift of God: not of works, lest any man should boast." The faith of Christ in us is a gift. And salvation comes as a free gift, *by grace—through faith*! But Paul explains that even the faith must be a gift. Otherwise, it would be a "work" generated by human effort. (You may wish to read our booklet *What Is Real Faith?* to better understand this subject.)

It is the very faith of Christ that works in a Christian. But grasp this. It *does* assist in performing works in all those who are led by God's Spirit. Expect God's help.

Almost universally, theologians, religionists and churchmen stop reading after Ephesians 2:8-9 ("by grace are you saved through faith; and that not of yourselves: it is the gift of God: not of works, lest any man should boast") and ignore vitally important verse 10: "For we are *His workmanship*, created in Christ Jesus *unto good works*, which God has before ordained that we should *walk in them*." That is right! Christians must "walk...in good works" as "His [God's] workmanship," overcoming daily.

Christ at Work

Quite literally, Jesus Christ lives His life in the Christian. Without His help, you will get nowhere—fast! You must exercise the fruit of faith from God's Spirit (Gal. 5:22-23), knowing that Christ is at work in you—if you are striving to yield to Him and doing all that you are capable of carrying out.

In John 15:5, Christ said, "bring forth much fruit" and then stated, "...for without Me you can do *nothing*." Human power—human energy—only helps a person overcome in *physical* areas. SPIRITUAL problems cannot be conquered through *physical* effort.

Christ is the Vine and we are the branches (John 15:5). The branches must be *connected* to the Vine. This happens through God's Spirit working in your mind.

When speaking of the way God's Spirit works, Jesus said, "out of his belly shall *flow rivers of living water.* (But this spoke He of *the Spirit*, which they that believe on Him should receive...)" (John 7:38). As it performs good works, God's Spirit flows "out of" the Christian. It does good works. Therefore, it *must* be replenished, or it will be depleted and disappear completely. This is why Jesus also said, "If you...know how to give good gifts unto your children: how much more shall your heavenly Father *give the Holy Spirit to them that ask Him?*" (Luke 11:13). You must regularly ask, in prayer, for more of the Holy Spirit.

Paul wrote, "my brethren, be strong in the Lord, and in the *power of His might*" (Eph. 6:10). Christ also said, "with God *all things are possible*" (Matt. 19:26). With God's Spirit actively working and growing in you, this can also be true of you! Exercise the faith of Christ as you work on yourself.

And remember! Deep conversion does not occur overnight. Paul wrote to the Corinthians that they were "babes [babies] in Christ" (I Cor. 3:1). He described how they required "milk," instead of "meat," for food. The brand new Christian is much like an infant. By analogy, he first learns to roll over, then crawl, before walking (and, at first, in an unsteady, toddling fashion). Only later does he finally learn to run (spiritually).

Paul compares conversion to running a race (I Cor. 9:24). At some point, the runner must develop great speed, because Paul says, "run, that you may obtain [win]."

Such is the Christian way of life. Slow, steady growth, through daily practice, produces progress in the life of the person who is copying Christ. The new Christian sincerely strives, from the heart, to be different—to turn around and go the other way, the way of God, for the rest of his life!

Apply yourself! Push yourself to grow and overcome. Do not expect it to be easy, like "falling off a log." Grow in knowledge as well (II Pet. 3:18).

Resisting Temptation

Christ taught His disciples to *understand* the pulls of human nature at work within them. When He taught, "That which comes out of the man, that defiles the man. For from within, out of the heart of men, proceed evil thoughts, adulteries, fornications, murders, thefts, covetousness, wickedness, deceit, lasciviousness, an evil eye, blasphemy, pride, foolishness" (Mark 7:20-22).

These same attitudes, pulls of the flesh and wrong patterns of conduct are also at work within you and me. They leave us fertile for temptation by Satan.

Therefore, many kinds of trials, tests and temptations will be thrown at you all through life. You must successfully resist them. They will often come when you least expect them. The devil will try to strike you where you are weakest—most vulnerable—least prepared. You must be on guard at all times—in a constant state of readiness! Do not assume you are stronger or more prepared than you think. Consider this: "Wherefore let him that thinks he stands take heed lest he fall" (I Cor. 10:12).

James explained how temptation can turn into sin: "But every man is tempted, when he is drawn away of his own lust, and enticed. Then when lust has conceived, it brings forth sin: and sin, when it is finished, brings forth death" (1:14-15). Put out wrong thoughts. Do not ease up or assume victory before they are gone!

Peter added, "Be sober, be *vigilant*; because your adversary the devil, as a roaring lion, walks about, seeking whom he may devour" (I Pet. 5:8). And James also instructed, "*Submit* yourselves therefore to God. *Resist the devil*, and he will flee from you" (4:7). Peter continued, "Whom resist steadfast in the faith, knowing that the same afflictions are accomplished *in your brethren that are in the world*" (I Pet. 5:9).

The second part of this verse offers encouragement: You are not alone in your struggle to overcome sin. All human beings face the same problems. Understand! "All have sinned" (Rom. 3:23) and "sin is the transgression of the law" (I John 3:4). God promises that "sin shall *not* have dominion over you" (Rom. 6:14).

Here is how Paul explained forces at work within him: "For that which I do I allow not: for what I would, that do I not; but what I hate, that do I...For the good that I would I do not: but the evil which I would not, that I do" (Rom. 7:15, 19).

This pictures what we all face. When you feel like this, battle! Resist! Use God's power within you. Call out to Him for help and always remember that you must "Draw near to God, and He will draw near to you. Cleanse your hands, you sinners; and purify your hearts, you double minded" (James 4:8).

Certainly, fulfilling this verse in your own life is not an overnight process. It takes time and much effort.

Seek God through earnest, regular, believing prayer. Commune with God daily. Pray without ceasing (I Thes. 5:17-18). Study your Bible (Matt. 4:4). Drink it in as God's Word—as Him talking to you personally, in the same way prayers are you talking to Him!

Above all, do not become discouraged and give up when the temptation is severe and appears unrelenting. Never forget that "there has no temptation taken you but such as is common to man: but God is faithful, who will not suffer you to be tempted above that you are able; but will with the temptation also make a way to escape, that you may be able to bear it" (I Cor. 10:13).

This is God's sure promise to all who seek to overcome!

Christ Overcame and Qualified to Replace Satan

Resisting the temptation of the devil was central to Christ overcoming sin. Matthew 4 contains the account: "Then was Jesus led up of the Spirit...to be *tempted* of the devil" (vs. 1). The devil repeatedly *tempted* Christ, in various ways. Carefully read the account. At the end of several attempts by Satan to break Christ's will, the account climaxes.

You will notice that, after being offered all the kingdoms of the world, Christ rebuked Satan (vs. 10), stating, "Get you hence, Satan." This is a nice way of saying that Christ told the devil to "get out." At this point, the temptation ended and the devil departed. Christ had successfully resisted!

Be prepared to tell Satan to "Get out" of your life as often as you have to. Successfully resist him by submitting to God completely— in all things!

Christ passed a very real test! He overcame the world, His flesh and the devil in overcoming sin and qualifying to pay for the sins of the world.

Recall, when speaking of having overcome the world, Christ said, "Be of good cheer." You can overcome in the same way that Christ did.

Seven Steps to Permanent Change

Applying the following SEVEN BASIC STEPS will help you overcome problems that you face. They represent principles that will work in the process of overcoming no matter the size of the problem or problems that you face.

If you diligently apply them, they will be a formula that will help you to permanently overcome in your life.

(1) HONESTLY FACE THE PROBLEM. Many people will not squarely face their problems. They hide their eyes from reality. Jeremiah 17:9 declares, "The heart is deceitful above all things, and desperately wicked: who can know it?" Most people willingly deceive themselves about their problems. Honestly face your problems. Look them right in the eye and see them for what they are.

(2) DO NOT GET DISCOURAGED. It is very easy to get discouraged now that you have acknowledged your problems. It is easy to be disheartened. This is natural. Be ready for this feeling to possibly strike you, after you have honestly faced the weakness, sin or fault that you are now ready to tackle. Paul wrote of those who are "troubled on every side, yet not distressed...perplexed, but not in despair" (II Cor. 4:8-9). You may feel this way as you face your problems, but do not get discouraged. Move on to the next step.

(3) SET YOUR WILL. Absolutely determine that you are going to defeat each particular problem and that each will *not defeat you*! Take a do-or-die approach to the battle that lies before you. It has been said that the hardest battle is the *first* battle. Set your will to address each sin or weakness successfully. Tell yourself that you are going to defeat it—that you are going to rip it from your character.

But recognize that you cannot fight the battle on your own. You must move to step four.

(4) FORM A PARTNERSHIP WITH GOD. If you set out to overcome on human strength alone, you will fail. That is assured. We have already touched on this. Paul wrote, "I can do *all things through Christ* which strengthens me" (Phil. 4:13). Jesus said, "I can of My own self do nothing" (John 5:30). On another occasion, when speaking to His disciples and talking about those who have certain things to overcome, Christ also said, "With men this is impossible; but *with God all things are possible*" (Matt. 19:26). Simply believe Christ's words. If He could do nothing on His own, neither can you or I. Be sure that you have formed a partnership with God and are not working on your own.

(5) START RIGHT WHERE YOU ARE. Admit that the problem is whatever size that it is. Neither overstate nor understate it. If it is a BIG problem, admit it! This is part of honestly facing it. If you are trying to overcome any pull of the flesh or temptation that has existed for a long time—that has been part of you for many years, even a lifetime—admit the size of the problem. It has been said, "The longest journey begins with a single step." That is true for the Christian. No matter how long it takes, or where you are when you start, start wherever you find yourself. If you have wasted time in deciding to address the problem, admit it. Acknowledge where you are and "Redeem the time" (Eph. 5:16).

(6) BE WILLING TO PAY THE PRICE. The Bible describes some who "grow weary" and "faint in the day of adversity" (Prov. 24:10). Solomon wrote that "their strength is small." Paul wrote, "And let us not be weary in well doing: for in due season we shall reap, if we faint not" (Gal. 6:9). Everything of value in life comes at a cost—a price. Sometimes this involves pain, suffering. Pay the price. Paul wrote that even Christ "learned obedience by the things which He suffered" (Heb. 5:8). None of us enjoy pain, but sometimes it is inescapable in the overcoming process. The Psalmist said, "Before I was afflicted I went astray: but now have I kept Your word" (Psa. 119:67). Four verses later, he added, "It is good for me that I have been afflicted; that I might learn Your statutes" (vs. 71).

(7) DO NOT GIVE UP BEFORE YOU HAVE SUCCEEDED. Paul talked of running in a race and finishing his course. He said that he "pressed toward the mark" (Phil. 3:13) on his way to the kingdom of God. Solomon wrote, "For a just man falls seven times, and rises up again"

(Prov. 24:16). Do not give up. Do not *EVER* give up! Wrestle, battle and struggle until you have completely overcome whatever obstacle, weakness, sin or problem you are facing!

Follow these points, always employing one step at a time. They have helped many to win the war of overcoming!

A Lifelong Battle

Recall that "He that *endures* to the end shall be SAVED." Living a life of growing and overcoming is not easy. It is a constant, daily struggle against the pulls of the flesh and the temptations of sin. But we are now being judged.

Peter wrote, "For the time is come that judgment must begin at the house of God: and if it first begin at us, what shall the end be of them that *obey not* the gospel of God? And *if the righteous scarcely be saved*, where shall the ungodly and the sinner appear?" (I Pet. 4:17-18).

Paul recognized that he—his words, deeds and thoughts—was being judged. Notice: "And this I do...that I might be partaker thereof with you. Know you not [most do not] that they which run in a RACE run all, but *one* receives the prize? So *run*, that you may obtain [win]. And every man that strives for the mastery [championship or victory] is temperate in all things. Now they [non-Christians] do it to obtain a corruptible crown; but we [Christians] an incorruptible. I therefore so RUN, not as uncertainly; so FIGHT I...lest that by any means, when I have preached to others, I myself should be a castaway [failure, loser]" (I Cor. 9:23-27) and "Wherefore...let us lay aside every weight, and the sin which does so easily beset us, and let us RUN WITH PATIENCE the RACE that is set before us" (Heb. 12:1).

Paul fought mightily against sin. He saw two opposing forces at work within his own mind. Notice the intensity with which he struggled to overcome the pulls within him: "For I know that in me (that is, in my flesh,) dwells no good thing: for *to will is present with me*; but how to perform that which is good I find not...I find then a law, that, when I would do good, evil is present with me. For I delight in the law of God after the inward man: but I see another law in my members, warring against the law of my mind, and bringing me into captivity to the law of sin which is in my members" (Rom. 7:18, 21-23).

He described Christianity as "wrestling" against the "wiles of the devil" (Eph. 6:11-12)—all who have wrestled understand how physically grueling this sport can be. And he instructed the Philippians to "PRESS toward the mark for the *prize* of the high calling of God in Christ Jesus" (3:14). He recognized that it takes great effort to run and win a long race.

Paul's overcoming represents a classic example of how one of God's greatest servants fought to overcome sin. At the end of his life, he was able to say that he had "fought the good fight" and that he had "run his course" knowing that a "crown" awaited him. But this did not happen without much wrestling, pressing, running, fighting and warring against the human nature that he strove to overcome.

But he also understood that his race was a marathon, not a sprint. So is yours.

A Lifetime Effort

If you are an adult, it took you 15 to 20 years just to grow to a certain height. This long, physical growth process probably included a number of "growing pains." No doubt, you fell and skinned your knee or bloodied your nose many times before you reached adulthood. *Christianity is no different!* Do not become discouraged and quit growing, any more than a child should become discouraged and "quit life" simply because he may have fallen down or skinned a knee. When your child falls, you tell him to get up, because it is part of life. *Christianity is no different!*

Children always want to grow up faster than life's timetable allows. Though childhood is wonderful in so many ways, it seems that most young people cannot wait for adulthood. *Christianity is no different!* But full, mature Christian adulthood only comes after a long period of practicing the right way of life.

Perfection is a goal that carries with it a way of life that must govern one's every thought, action and word. God looks on the heart, the *intention* of a person who is yielded to Him. As long as he is spiritually growing and overcoming—and led by the Holy Spirit—he remains a converted, begotten son of God.

It is only through regular prayer, Bible study, meditation and even fasting (going without food and water for a period of time) that the Christian will be able to overcome the three foes that lie in wait for him every day of his life.

Eventually, all nations will sit before the God of the Bible. Some will have qualified to rule and some will not. Notice: "When the Son of Man shall come in His glory, and all the holy angels with Him, then shall He sit *upon the throne of His glory*: and before Him shall be gathered *all nations*: and He shall separate them one from another, as a shepherd divides his *sheep* from the *goats*: and He shall set the sheep on His right hand, but the goats on the left. Then shall the King say unto them on His right hand, Come, you blessed of My Father, INHERIT THE KINGDOM prepared for you [all those who have overcome] from the foundation of the world" (Matt. 25:31-34).

The GOVERNMENT of God will soon be restored to Earth, and all who have prepared themselves will "inherit the kingdom." Only the *overcomers*, those who successfully submitted to God and resisted Satan throughout their lives, shall take part in this glorious future: "He that OVERCOMES shall *inherit all things*; and I will be his God, and he shall be My son. But the fearful, and unbelieving, and the abominable, and murderers, and whoremongers, and sorcerers, and idolaters, and all liars, shall have their part in the lake which burns with fire and brimstone: which is the second death" (Rev. 21:7-8).

How to Prevent Sin

In his article "How to Prevent Sin," Herbert W. Armstrong concluded with the following. Notice the important key he described. It will also help you:

"The way to put a thing OUT of the mind is to put an *opposite* thought IN the mind. So often I have noticed parents of babies strive so hard to 'shush' up the baby when it is crying. There's either something causing pain, which should be removed, or something is in the baby's mind that is causing its crying or fretting. Just saying 'shush!' or commanding the baby to stop fussing doesn't usually get very good results. We have reared four children, and long ago I learned the trick of quieting the baby by *getting its mind on something else*. Instead of commanding it to stop crying, attract its attention with some new object—get it interested in playing with that object...and before you know it the child will forget all about its crying.

"Try using this same method on yourself. But instead of material or worldly things, a mature person should use self-discipline and set his mind on spiritual things. Open your Bible. Put the study of some *spiritual* subject in your mind. Next time you are tempted, try it. Pray over it. Ask God to help you. See how rapidly you begin to win the victory over temptation and sin, and how marvelous will be your spiritual and CHARACTER growth."

Mr. Armstrong concluded a related article "How to be an Overcomer" with the following:

"If we draw nigh to God, and then KEEP close to Him, our problem will be solved. We will then have the FAITH. We will then be FILLED with His Spirit—His power to overcome.

"We can keep in spiritual training only if we keep our affections—our minds—our thoughts—on SPIRITUAL things. Read Col. 3:1-10. Most of us keep our minds filled with earthly, material cares and interests, turning to the spiritual only occasionally! Seek FIRST the Kingdom of God and HIS RIGHTEOUSNESS!

"Sometimes it takes a siege of FASTING AND PRAYER—earnest, *determined, persevering prayer*—*seeking* God with all our might—with weeping—staying with it, DETERMINED, until we get through. Then we must keep in CONTINUOUS prayer. Cast ALL our cares upon HIM. We are not doing that. If we do, there will be many things each day to pray about! And it takes daily PRIVATE prayer, in real earnest, besides family prayer. Is eternal life WORTH IT?"

God's Word Points the Way

A final quote from Mr. Armstrong sums up this book. It is taken from his "Personal from the Editor" in *Tomorrow's World*, May-June, 1970:

"The world has rejected God's Law—GOD'S WAY. It has gone the WAY that has brought every curse on mankind. The WORLD TOMORROW will change all that. It will be RULED BY GOD'S LAW!

"To QUALIFY to become a King—a RULER in the KINGDOM OF GOD—you must come to really KNOW that Law. And the WHOLE BIBLE is a magnification—an elaboration of its principles. It is ONLY those who REPENT of their transgressions of God's great spiritual Law—the Ten Commandments—and who surrender to and accept as Savior JESUS CHRIST, who can become begotten children of GOD. No one is a true Christian until he has received THE HOLY SPIRIT of God (Rom. 8:9). That is God's gift. It imparts the very LIFE of God. It renews and opens the MIND to comprehend spiritual knowledge. It bestows the LOVE of God—divine, SPIRITUAL love. It imparts POWER. It instills FAITH.

"Then, once really CONVERTED—the entire direction of your life CHANGED—you must continually OVERCOME. There are three very tough things to overcome—your own SELF with the pull of human nature; the WORLD, with its customs, false teachings, wrong ways, wrong fellowships; and the invisible yet very real devil. You must GROW not only in spiritual grace, but in the KNOWLEDGE of Christ—the KNOWLEDGE in God's INSTRUCTION BOOK—the Holy Bible. You must study—understand it—live henceforth by its directions. It points THE WAY—WALK YE IN IT!"

Much Knowledge

This book has brought extraordinary understanding to you, knowledge presented by no other organization. It has thoroughly examined the subject of the Ten Commandments. You have seen that they are the Law of God, not the law of Moses—and that every one of them was ordained (though certainly not always kept) from the time of Creation. You have seen sin defined—Old Testament and New—and learned that every one of the Ten Commandments was referenced in the New Testament. You also learned that New Testament grace does not "free" people from obedience to laws that were always intended to be for more than merely the Jews or the Israelites.

What About You?

In the end, you have seen the beauty, logic and simplicity of each of God's ten commands. You have seen the many benefits to the world if all people kept them. You have seen that Christians must overcome and prevent sin. You have seen that the Ten Commandments were *not* "nailed to the cross" but are *required* for salvation.

When confronted with difficult choices, most take the easier path. Will you swim against the popular current of all others around you? Will you OBEY the God of the Bible? Will you come to be and then remain close to God? Will you strive to live by each of the Ten Commandments (and other laws and principles of God) every day of your life?

Will you overcome and INHERIT ALL THINGS?

Other Books by David C. Pack

- The Awesome Potential of Man
- Tomorrow's Wonderful World – An Inside View!
- Saturday or Sunday – Which Is the Sabbath?
- America and Britain in Prophecy
- The History of the True Church – Where Is It Today?
- The Trinity – Is God Three-In-One?
- Sex – Its Unknown Dimension
- Dating and Courtship – God's Way
- Train Your Children God's Way
- Herbert W. Armstrong – His Life in Proper Perspective
- The Bible's Difficult Scriptures Explained!

081010
CM

The Restored Church of God

P.O. Box 23295
Wadsworth, OH 44282
USA

P.O. Box 4064
St. Catharines, ON L2R 7S3
CANADA

Phone: (330) 334-2266
Fax: (330) 334-6513
E-mail: info@thercg.org
Web: www.thercg.org